The Journal of
a Voyage to Lisbon

Henry Fielding

Contents

Introduction To Several Works

When it was determined to extend the present edition of Fielding, not merely by the addition of Jonathan Wild to the three universally popular novels, but by two volumes of Miscellanies, there could be no doubt about at least one of the contents of these latter. The Journal of a Voyage to Lisbon, if it does not rank in my estimation anywhere near to Jonathan Wild as an example of our author's genius, is an invaluable and delightful document for his character and memory. It is indeed, as has been pointed out in the General Introduction to this series, our main source of indisputable information as to Fielding dans son naturel, and its value, so far as it goes, is of the very highest. The gentle and unaffected stoicism which the author displays under a disease which he knew well was probably, if not certainly, mortal, and which, whether mortal or not, must cause him much actual pain and discomfort of a kind more intolerable than pain itself; his affectionate care for his family; even little personal touches, less admirable, but hardly less pleasant than these, showing an Englishman's dislike to be "done" and an Englishman's determination to be treated with proper respect, are scarcely less noticeable and important on the biographical side than the unimpaired brilliancy of his satiric and yet kindly observation of life and character is on the side of literature.

There is, as is now well known since Mr. Dobson's separate edition of the Voyage, a little bibliographical problem about the first appearance of this Journal in 1755. The best known issue of that year is much shorter than the version inserted by Murphy and reprinted here, the passages omitted being chiefly those reflecting on the captain, etc., and so likely to seem invidious in a book published just after the author's death, and for the benefit, as was expressly announced, of his family. But the curious thing is that there is ANOTHER edition, of date so early that some argument is necessary to determine the priority, which does give these passages and is identical with the later or standard version. For satisfaction on this point, however, I must refer readers to Mr. Dobson himself.

There might have been a little, but not much, doubt as to a companion piece for the Journal; for indeed, after we close this (with or without its "Fragment on Bolingbroke"), the remainder of Fielding's work lies on a distinctly lower level of interest. It is still interesting, or it would not be given here. It still has—at least that part which here appears seems to its editor to have—interest intrinsic and "simple of itself." But it is impossible for anybody who speaks critically to deny that we now get into the region where work is more interesting because of its authorship than it would be if its authorship were different or unknown. To put the same thing in a sharper antithesis, Fielding is interesting, first of all, because he is the author of Joseph Andrews, of Tom Jones, of Amelia, of Jonathan Wild, of the Journal. His plays, his essays, his miscellanies generally are interesting, first of all, because they were written by Fielding.

Yet of these works, the Journey from this World to the Next (which, by a grim trick of fortune, might have served as a title for the more interesting Voyage with which we have yoked it) stands clearly first both in scale and merit. It is indeed very unequal, and as the author was to leave it unfinished, it is a pity that he did not leave it unfinished much sooner than he actually did. The first ten chapters, if of a kind of satire which has now grown rather obsolete for the nonce, are of a good kind and good in their kind; the history of the metempsychoses of Julian is of a less good kind, and less good in that kind. The date of composition of the piece is not known, but it appeared in the Miscellanies of 1743, and may represent almost any period of its author's development prior to that year. Its form was a very common form at the time, and continued to be so. I do not know that it is necessary to assign any very special origin to it, though Lucian, its chief practitioner, was evidently and almost avowedly a favorite study of Fielding's. The Spanish romancers, whether borrowing it from Lucian or not, had been fond of it; their French followers, of whom the chief were Fontenelle and Le Sage, had carried it northwards; the English essayists had almost from the beginning continued the process of acclimatization. Fielding therefore found it ready to his hand, though the present condition of this example would lead us to suppose that he did not find his hand quite ready to it. Still, in the actual "journey," there are touches enough of the master—not yet quite in his stage of mastery. It seemed particularly desirable not to close the series without some representation of the work to which Fielding gave the prime of his manhood, and from which, had he not, fortunately for English literature, been driven decidedly against his will, we had had in all probability no Joseph Andrews, and pretty certainly no Tom Jones. Fielding's periodical and dramatic work has been comparatively seldom reprinted, and has never yet been reprinted as a whole. The dramas indeed are open to two objections—the first, that they are not very "proper;" the second, and much more serious, that they do not redeem this want of propriety by the possession of any remarkable literary merit. Three (or two and part of a third) seemed to escape this double censure—the first two acts of the Author's Farce (practically a piece to themselves, for the Puppet Show which follows is almost entirely independent); the famous burlesque of Tom Thumb, which stands between the Rehearsal and the Critic, but nearer to the former; and Pasquin, the maturest example of Fielding's satiric work in drama. These accordingly have been selected; the rest I have read, and he who likes may read. I have read many worse things than even the worst of them, but not often worse things by so good a writer as Henry Fielding. The next question concerned the selection of writings more miscellaneous still, so as to give in little a complete idea of Fielding's various powers and experiments. Two difficulties beset this part of the task—want of space and the absence of anything so markedly good as absolutely to insist on inclusion. The Essay on Conversation, however, seemed pretty peremptorily to challenge a place. It is in a style which Fielding was very slow to abandon, which indeed has left strong traces even on his great novels; and if its mannerism is not now very attractive, the separate traits in it are often sharp and well-drawn. The book would not have been complete without a specimen or two of Fielding's journalism. The Champion, his first attempt of this kind, has not been drawn upon in consequence of the extreme difficulty of fixing with absolute certainty on Fielding's part in it. I do not know whether political prejudice interferes, more than I have usually found it interfere, with my judgment of the two Hanoverian-partisan papers of the '45 time. But they certainly seem to me to fail in redeeming their dose of rancor and misrepresentation by any sufficient evidence of genius such as, to my taste, saves not only the party journalism in verse and prose of Swift and Canning and Praed on one side, but that of Wolcot and Moore and Sydney Smith on the other. Even the often-quoted journal of events in London under the Chevalier is overwrought and tedious. The best thing in the True Patriot seems to me to be Parson Adams' letter describing his adventure with a young "bowe" of his day; and this I select, together with one or two numbers of the Covent Garden Journal. I have not found in this latter anything more characteristic than Murphy's selection, though Mr. Dobson, with his unfailing kindness, lent me an original and unusually complete set of the Journal itself.

It is to the same kindness that I owe the opportunity of presenting the reader with something indisputably Fielding's and very characteristic of him, which Murphy did not print, and which has not, so far as I know, ever appeared either in a collection or a selection of Fielding's work. After the success of David Simple, Fielding gave his sister, for whom he had already written a preface to that novel, another preface for a set of Familiar Letters between the characters of David Simple and others. This preface Murphy reprinted; but he either did not notice, or did not choose to attend to, a note towards the end of the book attributing certain of the letters to the author of the preface, the attribution being accompanied by an agreeably warm and sisterly denunciation of those who ascribed to Fielding matter unworthy of him. From these the letter which I have chosen, describing a row on the Thames, seems to me not only characteristic, but, like all this miscellaneous work, interesting no less for its weakness than for its strength. In hardly any other instance known to me can we trace so clearly the influence of a suitable medium and form on the genius of the artist. There are some writers—Dryden is perhaps the greatest of them—to whom form and medium seem almost indifferent, their all-round craftsmanship being such that they can turn any kind and every style to their purpose. There are others, of whom I think our present author is the chief, who are never really at home but in one kind. In Fielding's case that kind was narrative of a peculiar sort, half-sentimental, half-satirical, and almost wholly sympathetic—narrative which has the singular gift of portraying the liveliest character and yet of admitting the widest disgression and soliloquy.

Until comparatively late in his too short life, when he found this special path of his (and it is impossible to say whether the actual finding was in the case of Jonathan or in the case of Joseph), he did but flounder and slip. When he had found it, and was content to walk in it, he strode with as sure and steady a step as any other, even the greatest, of those who carry and hand on the torch of literature through the ages. But it is impossible to derive full satisfaction from his feats in this part of the race without some notion of his performances elsewhere; and I believe that such a notion will be supplied to the readers of his novels by the following volumes, in a very large number of cases, for the first time.

Dedication To The Public

Your candor is desired on the perusal of the following sheets, as they are the product of a genius that has long been your delight and entertainment. It must be acknowledged that a lamp almost burnt out does not give so steady and uniform a light as when it blazes in its full vigor; but yet it is well known that by its wavering, as if struggling against its own dissolution, it sometimes darts a ray as bright as ever. In like manner, a strong and lively genius will, in its last struggles, sometimes mount aloft, and throw forth the most striking marks of its original luster.

Wherever these are to be found, do you, the genuine patrons of extraordinary capacities, be as liberal in your applauses of him who is now no more as you were of him whilst he was yet amongst you. And, on the other hand, if in this little work there should appear any traces of a weakened and decayed life, let your own imaginations place before your eyes a true picture in that of a hand trembling in almost its latest hour, of a body emaciated with pains, yet struggling for your entertainment; and let this affecting picture open each tender heart, and call forth a melting tear, to blot out whatever failings may be found in a work begun in pain, and finished almost at the same period with life. It was thought proper by the friends of the deceased that this little piece should come into your hands as it came from the hands of the author, it being judged that you would be better pleased to have an opportunity of observing the faintest traces of a genius you have long admired, than have it patched by a different hand, by which means the marks of its true author might have been effaced. That the success of the last written, though first published, volume of the author's posthumous pieces may be attended with some convenience to those innocents he hath left behind, will no doubt be a motive to encourage its circulation through the kingdom, which will engage every future genius to exert itself for your pleasure. The principles and spirit which breathe in every line of the small fragment begun in answer to Lord Bolingbroke will unquestionably be a sufficient apology for its publication, although vital strength was wanting to finish a work so happily begun and so well designed. PREFACE THERE would not, perhaps, be a more pleasant or profitable study, among those which have their principal end in amusement, than that of travels or voyages, if they were wrote as they might be and ought to be, with a joint view to the entertainment and information of mankind. If the conversation of travelers be so eagerly sought after as it is, we may believe their books will be still more agreeable company, as they will in general be more instructive and more entertaining. But when I say the conversation of travelers is usually so welcome, I must be understood to mean that only of such as have had good sense enough to apply their peregrinations to a proper use, so as to acquire from them a real and valuable knowledge of men and things, both which are best known by comparison. If the customs and manners of men were everywhere the same, there would be no office so dull as that of a traveler, for the difference of hills, valleys, rivers, in short, the various views of which we may see the face of the earth, would scarce afford him a pleasure worthy of his labor; and surely it would give him very little opportunity of communicating any kind of entertainment or improvement to others.

To make a traveler an agreeable companion to a man of sense, it is necessary, not only that he should have seen much, but that he should have overlooked much of what he hath seen. Nature is not, any more than a great genius, always admirable in her productions, and therefore the traveler, who may be called her commentator, should not expect to find everywhere subjects worthy of his notice. It is certain, indeed, that one may be guilty of omission, as well as of the opposite extreme; but a fault on that side will be more easily pardoned, as it is better to be hungry than surfeited; and to miss your dessert at the table of a man whose gardens abound with the choicest fruits, than to have your taste affronted with every sort of trash that can be picked up at the green-stall or the wheel-barrow. If we should carry on the analogy between the traveler and the commentator, it is impossible to keep one's eye a moment off from the laborious much-read doctor Zachary Gray, of whose redundant notes on Hudibras I shall only say that it is, I am confident, the single book extant in which above five hundred authors are quoted, not one of which could be found in the collection of the late doctor Mead.

As there are few things which a traveler is to record, there are fewer on which he is to offer his observations: this is the office of the reader; and it is so pleasant a one, that he seldom chooses to have it taken from him, under the pretense of lending him assistance. Some occasions, indeed, there are, when proper observations are pertinent, and others when they are necessary; but good sense alone must point them out. I shall lay down only one general rule; which I believe to be of universal truth between relator and hearer, as it is between author and reader; this is, that the latter never forgive any observation of the former which doth not convey some knowledge that they are sensible they could not possibly have attained of themselves.

But all his pains in collecting knowledge, all his judgment in selecting, and all his art in communicating it, will not suffice, unless he can make himself, in some degree, an agreeable as well as an instructive companion. The highest instruction we can derive from the tedious tale of a dull fellow scarce ever pays us for our attention. There is nothing, I think, half so valuable as knowledge, and yet there is nothing which men will give themselves so little trouble to attain; unless it be, perhaps, that lowest degree of it which is the object of curiosity, and which hath therefore that active passion constantly employed in its service. This, indeed, it is in the power of every traveler to gratify; but it is the leading principle in weak minds only.

To render his relation agreeable to the man of sense, it is therefore necessary that the voyager should possess several eminent and rare talents; so rare indeed, that it is almost wonderful to see them ever united in the same person. And if all these talents must concur in the relator, they are certainly in a more eminent degree necessary to the writer; for here the narration admits of higher ornaments of style, and every fact and sentiment offers itself to the fullest and most deliberate examination. It would appear, therefore, I think, somewhat strange if such writers as these should be found extremely common; since nature hath been a most parsimonious distributor of her richest talents, and hath seldom bestowed many on the same person. But, on the other hand, why there should scarce exist a single writer of this kind worthy our regard; and, whilst there is no other branch of history (for this is history) which hath not exercised the greatest pens, why this alone should be overlooked by all men of great genius and erudition, and delivered up to the Goths and Vandals as their lawful property, is altogether as difficult to determine. And yet that this is the case, with some very few exceptions, is most manifest. Of these I shall willingly admit Burnet and Addison; if the former was not, perhaps, to be considered as a political essayist, and the latter as a commentator on the classics, rather than as a writer of travels; which last title, perhaps, they would both of them have been least ambitious to affect. Indeed, if these two and two or three more should be removed from the mass, there would remain such a heap of dullness behind, that the appellation of voyage-writer would not appear very desirable. I am not here unapprised that old Homer himself is by some considered as a voyage-writer; and, indeed, the beginning of his Odyssey may be urged to countenance that opinion, which I shall not controvert. But, whatever species of writing the Odyssey is of, it is surely at the head of that species, as much as the Iliad is of another; and so far the excellent Longinus would allow, I believe, at this day.

But, in reality, the Odyssey, the Telemachus, and all of that kind, are to the voyage-writing I here intend, what romance is to true history, the former being the confounder and corrupter of the latter. I am far from supposing that Homer, Hesiod, and the other ancient poets and mythologists, had any settled design to pervert and confuse the records of antiquity; but it is certain they have effected it; and for my part I must confess I should have honored and loved Homer more had he written a true history of his own times in humble prose, than those noble poems that have so justly collected the praise of all ages; for, though I read these with more admiration and astonishment, I still read Herodotus, Thucydides, and Xenophon with more amusement and more satisfaction. The original poets were not, however, without excuse. They found the limits of nature too straight for the immensity of their genius, which they had not room to exert without extending fact by fiction: and that especially at a time when the manners of men were too simple to afford that variety which they have since offered in vain to the choice of the meanest writers. In doing this they are again excusable for the manner in which they have done it.

Ut speciosa dehine miracula promant.

They are not, indeed, so properly said to turn reality into fiction, as fiction into reality. Their paintings are so bold, their colors so strong, that everything they touch seems to exist in the very manner they represent it; their portraits are so just, and their landscapes so beautiful, that we acknowledge the strokes of nature in both, without inquiring whether Nature herself, or her journeyman the poet, formed the first pattern of the piece. But other writers (I will put Pliny at their head) have no such pretensions to indulgence; they lie for lying sake, or in order insolently to impose the most monstrous improbabilities and absurdities upon their readers on their own authority; treating them as some fathers treat children, and as other fathers do laymen, exacting their belief of whatever they relate, on no other foundation than their own authority, without ever taking the pains or adapting their lies to human credulity, and of calculating them for the meridian of a common understanding; but, with as much weakness as wickedness, and with more impudence often than either, they assert facts contrary to the honor of God, to the visible order of the creation, to the known laws of nature, to the histories of former ages, and to the experience of our own, and which no man can at once understand and believe. If it should be objected (and it can nowhere be objected better than where I now write,[12] as there is nowhere more pomp of bigotry) that whole nations have been firm believers in such most absurd suppositions, I reply, the fact is not true. They have known nothing of the matter, and have believed they knew not what. It is, indeed, with me no matter of doubt but that the pope and his clergy might teach any of those Christian heterodoxies, the tenets of which are the most diametrically opposite to their own; nay, all the doctrines of Zoroaster, Confucius, and Mahomet, not only with certain and immediate success, but without one Catholic in a thousand knowing he had changed his religion.

[12] At Lisbon.

What motive a man can have to sit down, and to draw forth a list of stupid, senseless, incredible lies upon paper, would be difficult to determine, did not Vanity present herself so immediately as the adequate cause. The vanity of knowing more than other men is, perhaps, besides hunger, the only inducement to writing, at least to publishing, at all. Why then should not the voyage-writer be inflamed with the glory of having seen what no man ever did or will see but himself? This is the true source of the wonderful in the discourse and writings, and sometimes, I believe, in the actions of men. There is another fault, of a kind directly opposite to this, to which these writers are sometimes liable, when, instead of filling their pages with monsters which nobody hath ever seen, and with adventures which never have, nor could possibly have, happened to them, waste their time and paper with recording things and facts of so common a kind, that they challenge no other right of being remembered than as they had the honor of having happened to the author, to whom nothing seems trivial that in any manner happens to himself.

Of such consequence do his own actions appear to one of this kind, that he would probably think himself guilty of infidelity should he omit the minutest thing in the detail of his journal. That the fact is true is sufficient to give it a place there, without any consideration whether it is capable of pleasing or surprising, of diverting or informing, the reader. I have seen a play (if I mistake not it is one of Mrs. Behn's or of Mrs. Centlivre's) where this vice in a voyage-writer is finely ridiculed. An ignorant pedant, to whose government, for I know not what reason, the conduct of a young nobleman in his travels is committed, and who is sent abroad to show my lord the world, of which he knows nothing himself, before his departure from a town, calls for his Journal to record the goodness of the wine and tobacco, with other articles of the same importance, which are to furnish the materials of a voyage at his return home. The humor, it is true, is here carried very far; and yet, perhaps, very little beyond what is to be found in writers who profess no intention of dealing in humor at all. Of one or other, or both of these kinds, are, I conceive, all that vast pile of books which pass under the names of voyages, travels, adventures, lives, memoirs, histories, etc., some of which a single traveler sends into the world in many volumes, and others are, by judicious booksellers, collected into vast bodies in folio, and inscribed with their own names, as if they were indeed their own travels: thus unjustly attributing to themselves the merit of others.

Now, from both these faults we have endeavored to steer clear in the following narrative; which, however the contrary may be insinuated by ignorant, unlearned, and fresh-water critics, who have never traveled either in books or ships, I do solemnly declare doth, in my own impartial opinion, deviate less from truth than any other voyage extant; my lord Anson's alone being, perhaps, excepted. Some few embellishments must be allowed to every historian; for we are not to conceive that the speeches in Livy, Sallust, or Thucydides, were literally spoken in the very words in which we now read them. It is sufficient that every fact hath its foundation in truth, as I do seriously aver is the ease in the ensuing pages; and when it is so, a good critic will be so far from denying all kind of ornament of style or diction, or even of circumstance, to his author, that he would be rather sorry if he omitted it; for he could hence derive no other advantage than the loss of an additional pleasure in the perusal.

Again, if any merely common incident should appear in this journal, which will seldom I apprehend be the case, the candid reader will easily perceive it is not introduced for its own sake, but for some observations and reflections naturally resulting from it; and which, if but little to his amusement, tend directly to the instruction of the reader or to the information of the public; to whom if I choose to convey such instruction or information with an air of joke and laughter, none but the dullest of fellows will, I believe, censure it; but if they should, I have the authority of more than one passage in Horace to allege in my defense. Having thus endeavored to obviate some censures, to which a man without the gift of foresight, or any fear of the imputation of being a conjurer, might conceive this work would be liable, I might now undertake a more pleasing task, and fall at once to the direct and positive praises of the work itself; of which indeed, I could say a thousand good things; but the task is so very pleasant that I shall leave it wholly to the reader, and it is all the task that I impose on him. A moderation for which he may think himself obliged to me when he compares it with the conduct of authors, who often fill a whole sheet with their own praises, to which they sometimes set their own real names, and sometimes a fictitious one. One hint, however, I must give the kind reader; which is, that if he should be able to find no sort of amusement in the book, he will be pleased to remember the public utility which will arise from it. If entertainment, as Mr. Richardson observes, be but a secondary consideration in a romance; with which Mr. Addison, I think, agrees, affirming the use of the pastry cook to be the first; if this, I say, be true of a mere work of invention, sure it may well be so considered in a work founded, like this, on truth; and where the political reflections form so distinguishing a part. But perhaps I may hear, from some critic of the most saturnine complexion, that my vanity must have made a horrid dupe of my judgment, if it hath flattered me with an expectation of having anything here seen in a grave light, or of conveying any useful instruction to the public, or to their guardians. I answer, with the great man whom I just now quoted, that my purpose is to convey instruction in the vehicle of entertainment; and so to bring about at once, like the revolution in the Rehearsal, a perfect reformation of the laws relating to our maritime affairs: an undertaking, I will not say more modest, but surely more feasible, than that of reforming a whole people, by making use of a vehicular story, to wheel in among them worse manners than their own.

Introduction

In the beginning of August, 1753, when I had taken the duke of Portland's medicine, as it is called, near a year, the effects of which had been the carrying off the symptoms of a lingering imperfect gout, I was persuaded by Mr. Ranby, the king's premier sergeant-surgeon, and the ablest advice, I believe, in all branches of the physical profession, to go immediately to Bath. I accordingly wrote that very night to Mrs. Bowden, who, by the next post, informed me she had taken me a lodging for a month certain. Within a few days after this, whilst I was preparing for my journey, and when I was almost fatigued to death with several long examinations, relating to five different murders, all committed within the space of a week, by different gangs of street-robbers, I received a message from his grace the duke of Newcastle, by Mr. Carrington, the king's messenger, to attend his grace the next morning, in Lincoln's-inn-fields, upon some business of importance; but I excused myself from complying with the message, as, besides being lame, I was very ill with the great fatigues I had lately undergone added to my distemper.

His grace, however, sent Mr. Carrington, the very next morning, with another summons; with which, though in the utmost distress, I immediately complied; but the duke, happening, unfortunately for me, to be then particularly engaged, after I had waited some time, sent a gentleman to discourse with me on the best plan which could be invented for putting an immediate end to those murders and robberies which were every day committed in the streets; upon which I promised to transmit my opinion, in writing, to his grace, who, as the gentleman informed me, intended to lay it before the privy council.

Though this visit cost me a severe cold, I, notwithstanding, set myself down to work; and in about four days sent the duke as regular a plan as I could form, with all the reasons and arguments I could bring to support it, drawn out in several sheets of paper; and soon received a message from the duke by Mr. Carrington, acquainting me that my plan was highly approved of, and that all the terms of it would be complied with. The principal and most material of those terms was the immediately depositing six hundred pound in my hands; at which small charge I undertook to demolish the then reigning gangs, and to put the civil policy into such order, that no such gangs should ever be able, for the future, to form themselves into bodies, or at least to remain any time formidable to the public.

I had delayed my Bath journey for some time, contrary to the repeated advice of my physical acquaintance, and to the ardent desire of my warmest friends, though my distemper was now turned to a deep jaundice; in which case the Bath waters are generally reputed to be almost infallible. But I had the most eager desire of demolishing this gang of villains and cut-throats, which I was sure of accomplishing the moment I was enabled to pay a fellow who had undertaken, for a small sum, to betray them into the hands of a set of thief-takers whom I had enlisted into the service, all men of known and approved fidelity and intrepidity.

After some weeks the money was paid at the treasury, and within a few days after two hundred pounds of it had come to my hands, the whole gang of cut-throats was entirely dispersed, seven of them were in actual custody, and the rest driven, some out of the town, and others out of the kingdom. Though my health was now reduced to the last extremity, I continued to act with the utmost vigor against these villains; in examining whom, and in taking the depositions against them, I have often spent whole days, nay, sometimes whole nights, especially when there was any difficulty in procuring sufficient evidence to convict them; which is a very common case in street-robberies, even when the guilt of the party is sufficiently apparent to satisfy the most tender conscience. But courts of justice know nothing of a cause more than what is told them on oath by a witness; and the most flagitious villain upon earth is tried in the same manner as a man of the best character who is accused of the same crime. Meanwhile, amidst all my fatigues and distresses, I had the satisfaction to find my endeavors had been attended with such success that this hellish society were almost utterly extirpated, and that, instead of reading of murders and street-robberies in the news almost every morning, there was, in the remaining part of the month of November, and in all December, not only no such thing as a murder, but not even a street-robbery committed. Some such, indeed, were mentioned in the public papers; but they were all found on the strictest inquiry, to be false. In this entire freedom from street-robberies, during the dark months, no man will, I believe, scruple to acknowledge that the winter of 1753 stands unrivaled, during a course of many years; and this may possibly appear the more extraordinary to those who recollect the outrages with which it began. Having thus fully accomplished my undertaking, I went into the country, in a very weak and deplorable condition, with no fewer or less diseases than a jaundice, a dropsy, and an asthma, altogether uniting their forces in the destruction of a body so entirely emaciated that it had lost all its muscular flesh. Mine was now no longer what was called a Bath case; nor, if it had been so, had I strength remaining sufficient to go thither, a ride of six miles only being attended with an intolerable fatigue. I now discharged my lodgings at Bath, which I had hitherto kept. I began in earnest to look on my case as desperate, and I had vanity enough to rank myself with those heroes who, of old times, became voluntary sacrifices to the good of the public. But, lest the reader should be too eager to catch at the word VANITY, and should be unwilling to indulge me with so sublime a gratification, for I think he is not too apt to gratify me, I will take my key a pitch lower, and will frankly own that I had a stronger motive than the love of the public to push me on: I will therefore confess to him that my private affairs at the beginning of the winter had but a gloomy aspect; for I had not plundered the public or the poor of those sums which men, who are always ready to plunder both as much as they can, have been pleased to suspect me of taking: on the contrary, by composing, instead of inflaming the quarrels of porters and beggars (which I blush when I say hath not been universally practiced), and by refusing to take a shilling from a man who most undoubtedly would not have had another left, I had reduced an income of about five hundred pounds[13] a-year of the dirtiest money upon earth to little more than three hundred pounds; a considerable proportion of which remained with my clerk; and, indeed, if the whole had done so, as it ought, he would be but ill paid for sitting almost sixteen hours in the twenty-four in the most unwholesome, as well as nauseous air in the universe, and which hath in his case corrupted a good constitution without contaminating his morals.

[13] A predecessor of mine used to boast that he made one thousand pounds a-year in his office; but how he did this (if indeed he did it) is to me a secret. His clerk, now mine, told me I had more business than he had ever known there; I am sure I had as much as any man could do. The truth is, the fees are so very low, when any are due, and so much is done for nothing, that, if a single justice of peace had business enough to employ twenty clerks, neither he nor they would get much by their labor.

The public will not, therefore, I hope, think I betray a secret when I inform them that I received from the Government a yearly pension out of the public service money; which, I believe, indeed, would have been larger had my great patron been convinced of an error, which I have heard him utter more than once, that he could not indeed say that the acting as a principal justice of peace in Westminster was on all accounts very desirable, but that all the world knew it was a very lucrative office. Now, to have shown him plainly that a man must be a rogue to make a very little this way, and that he could not make much by being as great a rogue as he could be, would have required more confidence than, I believe, he had in me, and more of his conversation than he chose to allow me; I therefore resigned the office and the farther execution of my plan to my brother, who had long been myassistant. And now, lest the case between me and the reader should be the same in both instances as it was between me and the great man, I will not add another word on the subject.

But, not to trouble the reader with anecdotes, contrary to my own rule laid down in my preface, I assure him I thought my family was very slenderly provided for; and that my health began to decline so fast that I had very little more of life left to accomplish what I had thought of too late. I rejoiced therefore greatly in seeing an opportunity, as I apprehended, of gaining such merit in the eve of the public, that, if my life were the sacrifice to it, my friends might think they did a popular act in putting my family at least beyond the reach of necessity, which I myself began to despair of doing. And though I disclaim all pretense to that Spartan or Roman patriotism which loved the public so well that it was always ready to become a voluntary sacrifice to the public good, I do solemnly declare I have that love for my family.

After this confession therefore, that the public was not the principal deity to which my life was offered a sacrifice, and when it is farther considered what a poor sacrifice this was, being indeed no other than the giving up what I saw little likelihood of being able to hold much longer, and which, upon the terms I held it, nothing but the weakness of human nature could represent to me as worth holding at all; the world may, I believe, without envy, allow me all the praise to which I have any title. My aim, in fact, was not praise, which is the last gift they care to bestow; at least, this was not my aim as an end, but rather as a means of purchasing some moderate provision for my family, which, though it should exceed my merit, must fall infinitely short of my service, if I succeeded in my attempt. To say the truth, the public never act more wisely than when they act most liberally in the distribution of their rewards; and here the good they receive is often more to be considered than the motive from which they receive it. Example alone is the end of all public punishments and rewards. Laws never inflict disgrace in resentment, nor confer honor from gratitude. "For it is very hard, my lord," said a convicted felon at the bar to the late excellent judge Burnet, "to hang a poor man for stealing a horse." "You are not to be hanged sir," answered my ever-honored and beloved friend, "for stealing a horse, but you are to be hanged that horses may not be stolen." In like manner it might have been said to the late duke of Marlborough, when the parliament was so deservedly liberal to him, after the battle of Blenheim, "You receive not these honors and bounties on account of a victory past, but that other victories may be obtained."

I was now, in the opinion of all men, dying of a complication of disorders; and, were I desirous of playing the advocate, I have an occasion fair enough; but I disdain such an attempt. I relate facts plainly and simply as they are; and let the world draw from them what conclusions they please, taking with them the following facts for their instruction: the one is, that the proclamation offering one hundred pounds for the apprehending felons for certain felonies committed in certain places, which I prevented from being revived, had formerly cost the government several thousand pounds within a single year. Secondly, that all such proclamations, instead of curing the evil, had actually increased it; had multiplied the number of robberies; had propagated the worst and wickedest of perjuries; had laid snares for youth and ignorance, which, by the temptation of these rewards, had been sometimes drawn into guilt; and sometimes, which cannot be thought on without the highest horror, had destroyed them without it. Thirdly, that my plan had not put the government to more than three hundred pound expense, and had produced none of the ill consequences above mentioned; but, lastly, had actually suppressed the evil for a time, and had plainly pointed out the means of suppressing it for ever. This I would myself have undertaken, had my health permitted, at the annual expense of the above-mentioned sum.

After having stood the terrible six weeks which succeeded last Christmas, and put a lucky end, if they had known their own interests, to such numbers of aged and infirm valetudinarians, who might have gasped through two or three mild winters more, I returned to town in February, in a condition less despaired of by myself than by any of my friends. I now became the patient of Dr.

Ward, who wished I had taken his advice earlier. By his advice I was tapped, and fourteen quarts of water drawn from my belly. The sudden relaxation which this caused, added to my enervate, emaciated habit of body, so weakened me that within two days I was thought to be falling into the agonies of death. I was at the worst on that memorable day when the public lost Mr. Pelham. From that day I began slowly, as it were, to draw my feet out of the grave; till in two months' time I had again acquired some little degree of strength, but was again full of water. During this whole time I took Mr. Ward's medicines, which had seldom any perceptible operation. Those in particular of the diaphoretic kind, the working of which is thought to require a great strength of constitution to support, had so little effect on me, that Mr. Ward declared it was as vain to attempt sweating me as a deal board. In this situation I was tapped a second time. I had one quart of water less taken from me now than before; but I bore all the consequences of the operation much better. This I attributed greatly to a dose of laudanum prescribed by my surgeon. It first gave me the most delicious flow of spirits, and afterwards as comfortable a nap.

The month of May, which was now begun, it seemed reasonable to expect would introduce the spring, and drive of that winter which yet maintained its footing on the stage. I resolved therefore to visit a little house of mine in the country, which stands at Ealing, in the county of Middlesex, in the best air, I believe, in the whole kingdom, and far superior to that of Kensington Gravel-pits; for the gravel is here much wider and deeper, the place higher and more open towards the south, whilst it is guarded from the north wind by a ridge of hills, and from the smells and smoke of London by its distance; which last is not the fate of Kensington, when the wind blows from any corner of the east.

Obligations to Mr. Ward I shall always confess; for I am convinced that he omitted no care in endeavoring to serve me, without any expectation or desire of fee or reward.

The powers of Mr. Ward's remedies want indeed no unfair puffs of mine to give them credit; and though this distemper of the dropsy stands, I believe, first in the list of those over which he is always certain of triumphing, yet, possibly, there might be something particular in my case capable of eluding that radical force which had healed so many thousands. The same distemper, in different constitutions, may possibly be attended with such different symptoms, that to find an infallible nostrum for the curing any one distemper in every patient may be almost as difficult as to find a panacea for the cure of all.

But even such a panacea one of the greatest scholars and best of men did lately apprehend he had discovered. It is true, indeed, he was no physician; that is, he had not by the forms of his education acquired a right of applying his skill in the art of physic to his own private advantage; and yet, perhaps, it may be truly asserted that no other modern hath contributed so much to make his physical skill useful to the public; at least, that none hath undergone the pains of communicating this discovery in writing to the world. The reader, I think, will scarce need to be informed that the writer I mean is the late bishop of Cloyne, in Ireland, and the discovery that of the virtues of tar-water.

I then happened to recollect, upon a hint given me by the inimitable and shamefully-distressed author of the Female Quixote, that I had many years before, from curiosity only, taken a cursory view of bishop Berkeley's treatise on the virtues of tar-water, which I had formerly observed he strongly contends to be that real panacea which Sydenham supposes to have an existence in nature, though it yet remains undiscovered, and perhaps will always remain so.

Upon the reperusal of this book I found the bishop only asserting his opinion that tar-water might be useful in the dropsy, since he had known it to have a surprising success in the cure of a most stubborn anasarca, which is indeed no other than, as the word implies, the dropsy of the flesh; and this was, at that time, a large part of my complaint.

After a short trial, therefore, of a milk diet, which I presently found did not suit with my case, I betook myself to the bishop's prescription, and dosed myself every morning and evening with half a pint of tar-water.

It was no more than three weeks since my last tapping, and my belly and limbs were distended with water. This did not give me the worse opinion of tar-water; for I never supposed there could be any such virtue in tar-water as immediately to carry off a quantity of water already collected. For my delivery from this I well knew I must be again obliged to the trochar; and that if the tar-water did me any good at all it must be only by the slowest degrees; and that if it should ever get the better of my distemper it must be by the tedious operation of undermining, and not by a sudden attack and storm.

Some visible effects, however, and far beyond what my most sanguine hopes could with any modesty expect, I very soon experienced; the tar-water having, from the very first, lessened my illness, increased my appetite, and added, though in a very slow proportion, to my bodily strength. But if my strength had increased a little my water daily increased much more. So that, by the end of May, my belly became again ripe for the trochar, and I was a third time tapped; upon which, two very favorable symptoms appeared. I had three quarts of water taken from me less than had been taken the last time; and I bore the relaxation with much less (indeed with scarce any) faintness.

Those of my physical friends on whose judgment I chiefly depended seemed to think my only chance of life consisted in having the whole summer before me; in which I might hope to gather sufficient strength to encounter the inclemencies of the ensuing winter. But this chance began daily to lessen. I saw the summer mouldering away, or rather, indeed, the year passing away without intending to bring on any summer at all. In the whole month of May the sun scarce appeared three times. So that the early fruits came to the fullness of their growth, and to some appearance of ripeness, without acquiring any real maturity; having wanted the heat of the sun to soften and meliorate their juices. I saw the dropsy gaining rather than losing ground; the distance growing still shorter between the tappings. I saw the asthma likewise beginning again to become more troublesome. I saw the midsummer quarter drawing towards a close. So that I conceived, if the Michaelmas quarter should steal off in the same manner, as it was, in my opinion, very much to be apprehended it would, I should be delivered up to the attacks of winter before I recruited my forces, so as to be anywise able to withstand them.

I now began to recall an intention, which from the first dawnings of my recovery I had conceived, of removing to a warmer climate; and, finding this to be approved of by a very eminent physician, I resolved to put it into immediate execution. Aix in Provence was the place first thought on; but the difficulties of getting thither were insuperable. The Journey by land, beside the expense of it, was infinitely too long and fatiguing; and I could hear of no ship that was likely to set out from London, within any reasonable time, for Marseilles, or any other port in that part of the Mediterranean.

Lisbon was presently fixed on in its room. The air here, as it was near four degrees to the south of Aix, must be more mild and warm, and the winter shorter and less piercing.

It was not difficult to find a ship bound to a place with which we carry on so immense a trade. Accordingly, my brother soon informed me of the excellent accommodations for passengers which were to be found on board a ship that was obliged to sail for Lisbon in three days. I eagerly embraced the offer, notwithstanding the shortness of the time; and, having given my brother full power to contract for our passage, I began to prepare my family for the voyage with the utmost expedition.

But our great haste was needless; for the captain having twice put off his sailing, I at length invited him to dinner with me at Fordhook, a full week after the time on which he had declared, and that with many asseverations, he must and would weigh anchor.

He dined with me according to his appointment; and when all matters were settled between us, left me with positive orders to be on board the Wednesday following, when he declared he would fall down the river to Gravesend, and would not stay a moment for the greatest man in the world. He advised me to go to Gravesend by land, and there wait the arrival of his ship, assigning many reasons for this, every one of which was, as I well remember, among those that had before determined me to go on board near the Tower.

The Voyage

WEDNESDAY, June 26, 1754.—On this day the most melancholy sun I had ever beheld arose, and found me awake at my house at Fordhook. By the light of this sun I was, in my own opinion, last to behold and take leave of some of those creatures on whom I doted with a mother-like fondness, guided by nature and passion, and uncured and unhardened by all the doctrine of that philosophical school where I had learned to bear pains and to despise death. In this situation, as I could not conquer Nature, I submitted entirely to her, and she made as great a fool of me as she had ever done of any woman whatsoever; under pretense of giving me leave to enjoy, she drew me in to suffer, the company of my little ones during eight hours; and I doubt not whether, in that time, I did not undergo more than in all my distemper.

At twelve precisely my coach was at the door, which was no sooner told me than I kissed my children round, and went into it with some little resolution. My wife, who behaved more like a heroine and philosopher, though at the same time the tenderest mother in the world, and my eldest daughter, followed me; some friends went with us, and others here took their leave; and I heard my behavior applauded, with many murmurs and praises to which I well knew I had no title; as all other such philosophers may, if they have any modesty, confess on the like occasions.

In two hours we arrived in Rotherhithe, and immediately went on board, and were to have sailed the next morning; but, as this was the king's proclamation-day, and consequently a holiday at the custom-house, the captain could not clear his vessel till the Thursday; for these holidays are as strictly observed as those in the popish calendar, and are almost as numerous. I might add that both are opposite to the genius of trade, and consequently contra bonum publicum.

To go on board the ship it was necessary first to go into a boat; a matter of no small difficulty, as I had no use of my limbs, and was to be carried by men who, though sufficiently strong for their burden, were, like Archimedes, puzzled to find a steady footing. Of this, as few of my readers have not gone into wherries on the Thames, they will easily be able to form to themselves an idea. However, by the assistance of my friend, Mr. Welch, whom I never think or speak of but with love and esteem, I conquered this difficulty, as I did afterwards that of ascending the ship, into which I was hoisted with more ease by a chair lifted with pulleys. I was soon seated in a great chair in the cabin, to refresh myself after a fatigue which had been more intolerable, in a quarter of a mile's passage from my coach to the ship, than I had before undergone in a land-journey of twelve miles, which I had traveled with the utmost expedition.

This latter fatigue was, perhaps, somewhat heightened by an indignation which I could not prevent arising in my mind. I think, upon my entrance into the boat, I presented a spectacle of the highest horror. The total loss of limbs was apparent to all who saw me, and my face contained marks of a most diseased state, if not of death itself. Indeed, so ghastly was my countenance, that timorous women with child had abstained from my house, for fear of the ill consequences of looking at me. In this condition I ran the gauntlope (so I think I may justly call it) through rows of sailors and watermen, few of whom failed of paying their compliments to me by all manner of insults and jests on my misery. No man who knew me will think I conceived any personal resentment at this behavior; but it was a lively picture of that cruelty and inhumanity in the nature of men which I have often contemplated with concern, and which leads the mind into a train of very uncomfortable and melancholy thoughts. It may be said that this barbarous custom is peculiar to the English, and of them only to the lowest degree; that it is an excrescence of an uncontrolled licentiousness mistaken for liberty, and never shows itself in men who are polished and refined in such manner as human nature requires to produce that perfection of which it is susceptible, and to purge away that malevolence of disposition of which, at our birth, we partake in common with the savage creation. This may be said, and this is all that can be said; and it is, I am afraid, but little satisfactory to account for the inhumanity of those who, while they boast of being made after God's own image, seem to bear in their minds a resemblance of the vilest species of brutes; or rather, indeed, of our idea of devils; for I don't know that any brutes can be taxed with such malevolence. A sirloin of beef was now placed on the table, for which, though little better than carrion, as much was charged by the master of the little paltry ale-house who dressed it as would have been demanded for all the elegance of the King's Arms, or any other polite tavern or eating-house! for, indeed, the difference between the best house and the worst is, that at the former you pay largely for luxury, at the latter for nothing.

Thursday, June 27.—This morning the captain, who lay on shore at his own house, paid us a visit in the cabin, and behaved like an angry bashaw, declaring that, had he known we were not to be pleased, he would not have carried us for five hundred pounds. He added many asseverations that he was a gentleman, and despised money; not forgetting several hints of the presents which had been made him for his cabin, of twenty, thirty, and forty guineas, by several gentlemen, over and above the sum for which they had contracted. This behavior greatly surprised me, as I knew not how to account for it, nothing having happened since we parted from the captain the evening before in perfect good humor; and all this broke forth on the first moment of his arrival this morning. He did not, however, suffer my amazement to have any long continuance before he clearly showed me that all this was meant only as an apology to introduce another procrastination (being the fifth) of his weighing anchor, which was now postponed till Saturday, for such was his will and pleasure.

Besides the disagreeable situation in which we then lay, in the confines of Wapping and Rotherhithe, tasting a delicious mixture of the air of both these sweet places, and enjoying the concord of sweet sounds of seamen, watermen, fish-women, oyster-women, and of all the vociferous inhabitants of both shores, composing altogether a greater variety of harmony than Hogarth's imagination hath brought together in that print of his, which is enough to make a man deaf to look at—I had a more urgent cause to press our departure, which was, that the dropsy, for which I had undergone three tappings, seemed to threaten me with a fourth discharge before I should reach Lisbon, and when I should have nobody on board capable of performing the operation; but I was obliged to hearken to the voice of reason, if I may use the captain's own words, and to rest myself contented. Indeed, there was no alternative within my reach but what would have cost me much too dear. There are many evils in society from which people of the highest rank are so entirely exempt, that they have not the least knowledge or idea of them; nor indeed of the characters which are formed by them. Such, for instance, is the conveyance of goods and passengers from one place to another. Now there is no such thing as any kind of knowledge contemptible in itself; and, as the particular knowledge I here mean is entirely necessary to the well understanding and well enjoying this journal; and, lastly, as in this case the most ignorant will be those very readers whose amusement we chiefly consult, and to whom we wish to be supposed principally to write, we will here enter somewhat largely into the discussion of this matter; the rather, for that no ancient or modern author (if we can trust the catalogue of doctor Mead's library) hath ever undertaken it, but that it seems (in the style of Don Quixote) a task reserved for my pen alone.

When I first conceived this intention I began to entertain thoughts of inquiring into the antiquity of traveling; and, as many persons have performed in this way (I mean have traveled) at the expense of the public, I flattered myself that the spirit of improving arts and sciences, and of advancing useful and substantial learning, which so eminently distinguishes this age, and hath given rise to more speculative societies in Europe than I at present can recollect the names of—perhaps, indeed, than I or any other, besides their very near neighbors, ever heard mentioned—would assist in promoting so curious a work; a work begun with the same views, calculated for the same purposes, and fitted for the same uses, with the labors which those right honorable societies have so cheerfully undertaken themselves, and encouraged in others; sometimes with the highest honors, even with admission into their colleges, and with enrollment among their members.

From these societies I promised myself all assistance in their power, particularly the communication of such valuable manuscripts and records as they must be supposed to have collected from those obscure ages of antiquity when history yields us such imperfect accounts of the residence, and much more imperfect of the travels, of the human race; unless, perhaps, as a curious and learned member of the young Society of Antiquarians is said to have hinted his conjectures, that their residence and their travels were one and the same; and this discovery (for such it seems to be) he is said to have owed to the lighting by accident on a book, which we shall have occasion to mention presently, the contents of which were then little known to the society.

The king of Prussia, moreover, who, from a degree of benevolence and taste which in either case is a rare production in so northern a climate, is the great encourager of art and science, I was well assured would promote so useful a design, and order his archives to be searched on my behalf. But after well weighing all these advantages, and much meditation on the order of my work, my whole design was subverted in a moment by hearing of the discovery just mentioned to have been made by the young antiquarian, who, from the most ancient record in the world (though I don't find the society are all agreed on this point), one long preceding the date of the earliest modern collections, either of books or butterflies, none of which pretend to go beyond the flood, shows us that the first man was a traveler, and that he and his family were scarce settled in Paradise before they disliked their own home, and became passengers to another place. Hence it appears that the humor of traveling is as old as the human race, and that it was their curse from the beginning. By this discovery my plan became much shortened, and I found it only necessary to treat of the conveyance of goods and passengers from place to place; which, not being universally known, seemed proper to be explained before we examined into its original. There are indeed two different ways of tracing all things used by the historian and the antiquary; these are upwards and downwards.

The former shows you how things are, and leaves to others to discover when they began to be so. The latter shows you how things were, and leaves their present existence to be examined by others. Hence the former is more useful, the latter more curious. The former receives the thanks of mankind; the latter of that valuable part, the virtuosi.

In explaining, therefore, this mystery of carrying goods and passengers from one place to another, hitherto so profound a secret to the very best of our readers, we shall pursue the historical method, and endeavor to show by what means it is at present performed, referring the more curious inquiry either to some other pen or to some other opportunity.

Now there are two general ways of performing (if God permit) this conveyance, viz., by land and water, both of which have much variety; that by land being performed in different vehicles, such as coaches, caravans, wagons, etc.; and that by water in ships, barges, and boats, of various sizes and denominations. But, as all these methods of conveyance are formed on the same principles, they agree so well together, that it is fully sufficient to comprehend them all in the general view, without descending to such minute particulars as would distinguish one method from another.

Common to all of these is one general principle that, as the goods to be conveyed are usually the larger, so they are to be chiefly considered in the conveyance; the owner being indeed little more than an appendage to his trunk, or box, or bale, or at best a small part of his own baggage, very little care is to be taken in stowing or packing them up with convenience to himself; for the conveyance is not of passengers and goods, but of goods and passengers.

Secondly, from this conveyance arises a new kind of relation, or rather of subjection, in the society, by which the passenger becomes bound in allegiance to his conveyer. This allegiance is indeed only temporary and local, but the most absolute during its continuance of any known in Great Britain, and, to say truth, scarce consistent with the liberties of a free people, nor could it be reconciled with them, did it not move downwards; a circumstance universally apprehended to be incompatible to all kinds of slavery; for Aristotle in his Politics hath proved abundantly to my satisfaction that no men are born to be slaves, except barbarians; and these only to such as are not themselves barbarians; and indeed Mr. Montesquieu hath carried it very little farther in the case of the Africans; the real truth being that no man is born to be a slave, unless to him who is able to make him so.

Thirdly, this subjection is absolute, and consists of a perfect resignation both of body and soul to the disposal of another; after which resignation, during a certain time, his subject retains no more power over his own will than an Asiatic slave, or an English wife, by the laws of both countries, and by the customs of one of them. If I should mention the instance of a stage-coachman, many of my readers would recognize the truth of what I have here observed; all, indeed, that ever have been under the dominion of that tyrant, who in this free country is as absolute as a Turkish bashaw. In two particulars only his power is defective; he cannot press you into his service, and if you enter yourself at one place, on condition of being discharged at a certain time at another, he is obliged to perform his agreement, if God permit, but all the intermediate time you are absolutely under his government; he carries you how he will, when he will, and whither he will, provided it be not much out of the road; you have nothing to eat or to drink, but what, and when, and where he pleases. Nay, you cannot sleep unless he pleases you should; for he will order you sometimes out of bed at midnight and hurry you away at a moment's warning: indeed, if you can sleep in his vehicle he cannot prevent it; nay, indeed, to give him his due, this he is ordinarily disposed to encourage: for the earlier he forces yon to rise in the morning, the more time he will give you in the heat of the day, sometimes even six hours at an ale-house, or at their doors, where he always gives you the same indulgence which he allows himself; and for this he is generally very moderate in his demands. I have known a whole bundle of passengers charged no more than half-a-crown for being suffered to remain quiet at an ale-house door for above a whole hour, and that even in the hottest day in summer. But as this kind of tyranny, though it hath escaped our political writers, hath been I think touched by our dramatic, and is more trite among the generality of readers; and as this and all other kinds of such subjection are alike unknown to my friends, I will quit the passengers by land, and treat of those who travel by water; for whatever is said on this subject is applicable to both alike, and we may bring them together as closely as they are brought in the liturgy, when they are recommended to the prayers of all Christian congregations; and (which I have often thought very remarkable) where they are joined with other miserable wretches, such as women in labor, people in sickness, infants just born, prisoners and captives. Goods and passengers are conveyed by water in divers vehicles, the principal of which being a ship, it shall suffice to mention that alone. Here the tyrant doth not derive his title, as the stage-coachman doth, from the vehicle itself in which he stows his goods and passengers, but he is called the captain—a word of such various use and uncertain signification, that it seems very difficult to fix any positive idea to it: if, indeed, there be any general meaning which may comprehend all its different uses, that of the head or chief of any body of men seems to be most capable of this comprehension; for whether they be a company of soldiers, a crew of sailors, or a gang of rogues, he who is at the head of them is always styled the captain.

The particular tyrant whose fortune it was to stow us aboard laid a farther claim to this appellation than the bare command of a vehicle of conveyance. He had been the captain of a privateer, which he chose to call being in the king's service, and thence derived a right of hoisting the military ornament of a cockade over the button of his hat. He likewise wore a sword of no ordinary length by his side, with which he swaggered in his cabin, among the wretches his passengers, whom he had stowed in cupboards on each side. He was a person of a very singular character. He had taken it into his head that he was a gentleman, from those very reasons that proved he was not one; and to show himself a fine gentleman, by a behavior which seemed to insinuate he had never seen one. He was, moreover, a man of gallantry; at the age of seventy he had the finicalness of Sir Courtly Nice, with the roughness of Surly; and, while he was deaf himself, had a voice capable of deafening all others.

Now, as I saw myself in danger by the delays of the captain, who was, in reality, waiting for more freight, and as the wind had been long nested, as it were, in the southwest, where it constantly blew hurricanes, I began with great reason to apprehend that our voyage might be long, and that my belly, which began already to be much extended, would require the water to be let out at a time when no assistance was at hand; though, indeed, the captain comforted me with assurances that he had a pretty young fellow on board who acted as his surgeon, as I found he likewise did as steward, cook, butler, sailor. In short, he had as many offices as Scrub in the play, and went through them all with great dexterity; this of surgeon was, perhaps, the only one in which his skill was somewhat deficient, at least that branch of tapping for the dropsy; for he very ingenuously and modestly confessed he had never seen the operation performed, nor was possessed of that chirurgical instrument with which it is performed.

Friday, June 28.—By way of prevention, therefore, I this day sent for my friend, Mr. Hunter, the great surgeon and anatomist of Covent-garden; and, though my belly was not yet very full and tight, let out ten quarts of water; the young sea-surgeon attended the operation, not as a performer, but as a student.

I was now eased of the greatest apprehension which I had from the length of the passage; and I told the captain I was become indifferent as to the time of his sailing. He expressed much satisfaction in this declaration, and at hearing from me that I found myself, since my tapping, much lighter and better. In this, I believe, he was sincere; for he was, as we shall have occasion to observe more than once, a very good-natured man; and, as he was a very brave one too, I found that the heroic constancy with which I had borne an operation that is attended with scarce any degree of pain had not a little raised me in his esteem. That he might adhere, therefore, in the most religious and rigorous manner to his word, when he had no longer any temptation from interest to break it, as he had no longer any hopes of more goods or passengers, he ordered his ship to fall down to Gravesend on Sunday morning, and there to wait his arrival.

Sunday, June 30.—Nothing worth notice passed till that morning, when my poor wife, after passing a night in the utmost torments of the toothache, resolved to have it drawn. I despatched therefore a servant into Wapping to bring in haste the best tooth-drawer he could find. He soon found out a female of great eminence in the art;

but when he brought her to the boat, at the waterside, they were informed that the ship was gone; for indeed she had set out a few minutes after his quitting her; nor did the pilot, who well knew the errand on which I had sent my servant, think fit to wait a moment for his return, or to give me any notice of his setting out, though I had very patiently attended the delays of the captain four days, after many solemn promises of weighing anchor every one of the three last. But of all the petty bashaws or turbulent tyrants I ever beheld, this sour-faced pilot was the worst tempered; for, during the time that he had the guidance of the ship, which was till we arrived in the Downs, he complied with no one's desires, nor did he give a civil word, or indeed a civil look, to any on board.

The tooth-drawer, who, as I said before, was one of great eminence among her neighbors, refused to follow the ship; so that my man made himself the best of his way, and with some difficulty came up with us before we were got under full sail; for after that, as we had both wind and tide with us, he would have found it impossible to overtake the ship till she was come to an anchor at Gravesend.

The morning was fair and bright, and we had a passage thither, I think, as pleasant as can be conceived: for, take it with all its advantages, particularly the number of fine ships you are always sure of seeing by the way, there is nothing to equal it in all the rivers of the world. The yards of Deptford and of Woolwich are noble sights, and give us a just idea of the great perfection to which we are arrived in building those floating castles, and the figure which we may always make in Europe among the other maritime powers. That of Woolwich, at least, very strongly imprinted this idea on my mind; for there was now on the stocks there the Royal Anne, supposed to be the largest ship ever built, and which contains ten carriage-guns more than had ever yet equipped a first-rate.

It is true, perhaps, that there is more of ostentation than of real utility in ships of this vast and unwieldy burden, which are rarely capable of acting against an enemy; but if the building such contributes to preserve, among other nations, the notion of the British superiority in naval affairs, the expense, though very great, is well incurred, and the ostentation is laudable and truly political. Indeed, I should be sorry to allow that Holland, France, or Spain, possessed a vessel larger and more beautiful than the largest and most beautiful of ours; for this honor I would always administer to the pride of our sailors, who should challenge it from all their neighbors with truth and success. And sure I am that not our honest tars alone, but every inhabitant of this island, may exult in the comparison, when he considers the king of Great Britain as a maritime prince, in opposition to any other prince in Europe; but I am not so certain that the same idea of superiority will result from comparing our land forces with those of many other crowned heads. In numbers they all far exceed us, and in the goodness and splendor of their troops many nations, particularly the Germans and French, and perhaps the Dutch, cast us at a distance; for, however we may flatter ourselves with the Edwards and Henrys of former ages, the change of the whole art of war since those days, by which the advantage of personal strength is in a manner entirely lost, hath produced a change in military affairs to the advantage of our enemies. As for our successes in later days, if they were not entirely owing to the superior genius of our general, they were not a little due to the superior force of his money. Indeed, if we should arraign marshal Saxe of ostentation when he showed his army, drawn up, to our captive general, the day after the battle of La Val, we cannot say that the ostentation was entirely vain; since he certainly showed him an army which had not been often equaled, either in the number or goodness of the troops, and which, in those respects, so far exceeded ours, that none can ever cast any reflection on the brave young prince who could not reap the laurels of conquest in that day; but his retreat will be always mentioned as an addition to his glory.

In our marine the case is entirely the reverse, and it must be our own fault if it doth not continue so; for continue so it will as long as the flourishing state of our trade shall support it, and this support it can never want till our legislature shall cease to give sufficient attention to the protection of our trade, and our magistrates want sufficient power, ability, and honesty, to execute the laws; a circumstance not to be apprehended, as it cannot happen till our senates and our benches shall be filled with the blindest ignorance, or with the blackest corruption.

Besides the ships in the docks, we saw many on the water: the yachts are sights of great parade, and the king's body yacht is, I believe, unequaled in any country for convenience as well as magnificence; both which are consulted in building and equipping her with the most exquisite art and workmanship.

We saw likewise several Indiamen just returned from their voyage.

These are, I believe, the largest and finest vessels which are anywhere employed in commercial affairs. The colliers, likewise, which are very numerous, and even assemble in fleets, are ships of great bulk; and if we descend to those used in the American, African, and European trades, and pass through those which visit our own coasts, to the small craft that lie between Chatham and the Tower, the whole forms a most pleasing object to the eye, as well as highly warming to the heart of an Englishman who has any degree of love for his country, or can recognize any effect of the patriot in his constitution. Lastly, the Royal Hospital at Greenwich, which presents so delightful a front to the water, and doth such honor at once to its builder and the nation, to the great skill and ingenuity of the one, and to the no less sensible gratitude of the other, very properly closes the account of this scene; which may well appear romantic to those who have not themselves seen that, in this one instance, truth and reality are capable, perhaps, of exceeding the power of fiction. When we had passed by Greenwich we saw only two or three gentlemen's houses, all of very moderate account, till we reached Gravesend: these are all on the Kentish shore, which affords a much dryer, wholesomer, and pleasanter situation, than doth that of its opposite, Essex. This circumstance, I own, is somewhat surprising to me, when I reflect on the numerous villas that crowd the river from Chelsea upwards as far as Shepperton, where the narrower channel affords not half so noble a prospect, and where the continual succession of the small craft, like the frequent repetition of all things, which have nothing in them great, beautiful, or admirable, tire the eye, and give us distaste and aversion, instead of pleasure. With some of these situations, such as Barnes, Mortlake, etc., even the shore of Essex might contend, not upon very unequal terms; but on the Kentish borders there are many spots to be chosen by the builder which might justly claim the preference over almost the very finest of those in Middlesex and Surrey.

How shall we account for this depravity in taste? for surely there are none so very mean and contemptible as to bring the pleasure of seeing a number of little wherries, gliding along after one another, in competition with what we enjoy in viewing a succession of ships, with all their sails expanded to the winds, bounding over the waves before us.

And here I cannot pass by another observation on the deplorable want of taste in our enjoyments, which we show by almost totally neglecting the pursuit of what seems to me the highest degree of amusement; this is, the sailing ourselves in little vessels of our own, contrived only for our ease and accommodation, to which such situations of our villas as I have recommended would be so convenient, and even necessary.

This amusement, I confess, if enjoyed in any perfection, would be of the expensive kind; but such expense would not exceed the reach of a moderate fortune, and would fall very short of the prices which are daily paid for pleasures of a far inferior rate.

The truth, I believe, is, that sailing in the manner I have just mentioned is a pleasure rather unknown, or unthought of, than rejected by those who have experienced it; unless, perhaps, the apprehension of danger or seasickness may be supposed, by the timorous and delicate, to make too large deductions—insisting that all their enjoyments shall come to them pure and unmixed, and being ever ready to cry out,

— —Nocet empta dolore voluptas.

This, however, was my present case; for the ease and lightness which I felt from my tapping, the gayety of the morning, the pleasant sailing with wind and tide, and the many agreeable objects with which I was constantly entertained during the whole way, were all suppressed and overcome by the single consideration of my wife's pain, which continued incessantly to torment her till we came to an anchor, when I dispatched a messenger in great haste for the best reputed operator in Gravesend. A surgeon of some eminence now appeared, who did not decline tooth-drawing, though he certainly would have been offended with the appellation of tooth-drawer no less than his brethren, the members of that venerable body, would be with that of barber, since the late separation between those long-united companies, by which, if the surgeons have gained much, the barbers are supposed to have lost very little. This able and careful person (for so I sincerely believe he is) after examining the guilty tooth, declared that it was such a rotten shell, and so placed at the very remotest end of the upper jaw, where it was in a manner covered and secured by a large fine firm tooth, that he despaired of his power of drawing it.

He said, indeed, more to my wife, and used more rhetoric to dissuade her from having it drawn, than is generally employed to persuade young ladies to prefer a pain of three moments to one of three months' continuance, especially if those young ladies happen to be past forty and fifty years of age, when, by submitting to support a racking torment, the only good circumstance attending which is, it is so short that scarce one in a thousand can cry out "I feel it," they are to do a violence to their charms, and lose one of those beautiful holders with which alone Sir Courtly Nice declares a lady can ever lay hold of his heart. He said at last so much, and seemed to reason so justly, that I came over to his side, and assisted him in prevailing on my wife (for it was no easy matter) to resolve on keeping her tooth a little longer, and to apply palliatives only for relief. These were opium applied to the tooth, and blisters behind the ears.

Whilst we were at dinner this day in the cabin, on a sudden the window on one side was beat into the room with a crash as if a twenty-pounder had been discharged among us. We were all alarmed at the suddenness of the accident, for which, however, we were soon able to account, for the sash, which was shivered all to pieces, was pursued into the middle of the cabin by the bowsprit of a little ship called a cod-smack, the master of which made us amends for running (carelessly at best) against us, and injuring the ship, in the sea-way; that is to say, by damning us all to hell, and uttering several pious wishes that it had done us much more mischief. All which were answered in their own kind and phrase by our men, between whom and the other crew a dialogue of oaths and scurrility was carried on as long as they continued in each other's hearing.

It is difficult, I think, to assign a satisfactory reason why sailors in general should, of all others, think themselves entirely discharged from the common bands of humanity, and should seem to glory in the language and behavior of savages! They see more of the world, and have, most of them, a more erudite education than is the portion of landmen of their degree. Nor do I believe that in any country they visit (Holland itself not excepted) they can ever find a parallel to what daily passes on the river Thames. Is it that they think true courage (for they are the bravest fellows upon earth) inconsistent with all the gentleness of a humane carriage, and that the contempt of civil order springs up in minds but little cultivated, at the same time and from the same principles with the contempt of danger and death? Is it—? in short, it is so; and how it comes to be so I leave to form a question in the Robin Hood Society, or to he propounded for solution among the enigmas in the Woman's Almanac for the next year.

Monday, July 1.—This day Mr. Welch took his leave of me after dinner, as did a young lady of her sister, who was proceeding with my wife to Lisbon. They both set out together in a post-chaise for London. Soon after their departure our cabin, where my wife and I were sitting together, was visited by two ruffians, whose appearance greatly corresponded with that of the sheriffs, or rather the knight-marshal's bailiffs. One of these especially, who seemed to affect a more than ordinary degree of rudeness and insolence, came in without any kind of ceremony, with a broad gold lace on his hat, which was cocked with much military fierceness on his head. An inkhorn at his buttonhole and some papers in his hand sufficiently assured me what he was, and I asked him if he and his companion were not custom-house officers: he answered with sufficient dignity that they were, as an information which he seemed to conclude would strike the hearer with awe, and suppress all further inquiry; but, on the contrary, I proceeded to ask of what rank he was in the custom-house, and, receiving an answer from his companion, as I remember, that the gentleman was a riding surveyor, I replied that he might be a riding surveyor, but could be no gentleman, for that none who had any title to that denomination would break into the presence of a lady without an apology or even moving his hat. He then took his covering from his head and laid it on the table, saying, he asked pardon, and blamed the mate, who should, he said, have informed him if any persons of distinction were below. I told him he might guess by our appearance (which, perhaps, was rather more than could be said with the strictest adherence to truth) that he was before a gentleman and lady, which should teach him to be very civil in his behavior, though we should not happen to be of that number whom the world calls people of fashion and distinction. However, I said, that as he seemed sensible of his error, and had asked pardon, the lady would permit him to put his hat on again if he chose it. This he refused with some degree of surliness, and failed not to convince me that, if I should condescend to become more gentle, he would soon grow more rude. I now renewed a reflection, which I have often seen occasion to make, that there is nothing so incongruous in nature as any kind of power with lowness of mind and of ability, and that there is nothing more deplorable than the want of truth in the whimsical notion of Plato, who tells us that "Saturn, well knowing the state of human affairs, gave us kings and rulers, not of human but divine original; for, as we make not shepherds of sheep, nor oxherds of oxen, nor goatherds of goats, but place some of our own kind over all as being better and fitter to govern them; in the same manner were demons by the divine love set over us as a race of beings of a superior order to men, and who, with great ease to themselves, might regulate our affairs and establish peace, modesty, freedom, and justice, and, totally destroying all sedition, might complete the happiness of the human race. So far, at least, may even now be said with truth, that in all states which are under the government of mere man, without any divine assistance, there is nothing but labor and misery to be found. From what I have said, therefore, we may at least learn, with our utmost endeavors, to imitate the Saturnian institution; borrowing all assistance from our immortal part, while we pay to this the strictest obedience, we should form both our private economy and public policy from its dictates. By this dispensation of our immortal minds we are to establish a law and to call it by that name. But if any government be in the hands of a single person, of the few, or of the many, and such governor or governors shall abandon himself or themselves to the unbridled pursuit of the wildest pleasures or desires, unable to restrain any passion, but possessed with an insatiable bad disease; if such shall attempt to govern, and at the same time to trample on all laws, there can be no means of preservation left for the wretched people." Plato de Leg., lib. iv. p. 713, c. 714, edit. Serrani.

It is true that Plato is here treating of the highest or sovereign power in a state, but it is as true that his observations are general and may be applied to all inferior powers; and, indeed, every subordinate degree is immediately derived from the highest; and, as it is equally protected by the same force and sanctified by the same authority, is alike dangerous to the well-being of the subject. Of all powers, perhaps, there is none so sanctified and protected as this which is under our present consideration. So numerous, indeed, and strong, are the sanctions given to it by many acts of parliament, that, having once established the laws of customs on merchandise, it seems to have been the sole view of the legislature to strengthen the hands and to protect the persons of the officers who became established by those laws, many of whom are so far from bearing any resemblance to the Saturnian institution, and to be chosen from a degree of beings superior to the rest of human race, that they sometimes seem industriously picked out of the lowest and vilest orders of mankind. There is, indeed, nothing, so useful to man in general, nor so beneficial to particular societies and individuals, as trade. This is that alma mater at whose plentiful breast all mankind are nourished. It is true, like other parents, she is not always equally indulgent to all her children, but, though she gives to her favorites a vast proportion of redundancy and superfluity, there are very few whom she refuses to supply with the conveniences, and none with the necessaries, of life.

Such a benefactress as this must naturally be beloved by mankind in general; it would be wonderful, therefore, if her interest was not considered by them, and protected from the fraud and violence of some of her rebellious offspring, who, coveting more than their share or more than she thinks proper to allow them, are daily employed in meditating mischief against her, and in endeavoring to steal from their brethren those shares which this great alma mater had allowed them.

At length our governor came on board, and about six in the evening we weighed anchor, and fell down to the Nore, whither our passage was extremely pleasant, the evening being very delightful, the moon just past the full, and both wind and tide favorable to us.

Tuesday, July 2.—This morning we again set sail, under all the advantages we had enjoyed the evening before. This day we left the shore of Essex and coasted along Kent, passing by the pleasant island of Thanet, which is an island, and that of Sheppy, which is not an island, and about three o 'clock, the wind being now full in our teeth, we came to an anchor in the Downs, within two miles of Deal.—My wife, having suffered intolerable pain from her tooth, again renewed her resolution of having it drawn, and another surgeon was sent for from Deal, but with no better success than the former. He likewise declined the operation, for the same reason which had been assigned by the former: however, such was her resolution, backed with pain, that he was obliged to make the attempt, which concluded more in honor of his judgment than of his operation; for, after having put my poor wife to inexpressible torment, he was obliged to leave her tooth in statu quo; and she had now the comfortable prospect of a long fit of pain, which might have lasted her whole voyage, without any possibility of relief. In these pleasing sensations, of which I had my just share, nature, overcome with fatigue, about eight in the evening resigned her to rest—a circumstance which would have given me some happiness, could I have known how to employ those spirits which were raised by it; but, unfortunately for me, I was left in a disposition of enjoying an agreeable hour without the assistance of a companion, which has always appeared to me necessary to such enjoyment; my daughter and her companion were both retired sea-sick to bed; the other passengers were a rude school-boy of fourteen years old and an illiterate Portuguese friar, who understood no language but his own, in which I had not the least smattering. The captain was the only person left in whose conversation I might indulge myself; but unluckily, besides a total ignorance of everything in the world but a ship, he had the misfortune of being so deaf, that to make him hear, I will not say understand, my words, I must run the risk of conveying them to the ears of my wife, who, though in another room (called, I think, the state-room—being, indeed, a most stately apartment, capable of containing one human body in length, if not very tall, and three bodies in breadth), lay asleep within a yard of me. In this situation necessity and choice were one and the same thing; the captain and I sat down together to a small bowl of punch, over which we both soon fell fast asleep, and so concluded the evening.

Wednesday, July 3.—This morning I awaked at four o'clock for my distemper seldom suffered me to sleep later. I presently got up, and had the pleasure of enjoying the sight of a tempestuous sea for four hours before the captain was stirring; for he loved to indulge himself in morning slumbers, which were attended with a wind-music, much more agreeable to the performers than to the hearers, especially such as have, as I had, the privilege of sitting in the orchestra. At eight o'clock the captain rose, and sent his boat on shore. I ordered my man likewise to go in it, as my distemper was not of that kind which entirely deprives us of appetite. Now, though the captain had well victualled his ship with all manner of salt provisions for the voyage, and had added great quantities of fresh stores, particularly of vegetables, at Gravesend, such as beans and peas, which had been on board only two days, and had possibly not been gathered above two more, I apprehended I could provide better for myself at Deal than the ship's ordinary seemed to promise. I accordingly sent for fresh provisions of all kinds from the shore, in order to put off the evil day of starving as long as possible. My man returned with most of the articles I sent for, and I now thought myself in a condition of living a week on my own provisions. I therefore ordered my own dinner, which I wanted nothing but a cook to dress and a proper fire to dress it at; but those were not to be had, nor indeed any addition to my roast mutton, except the pleasure of the captain's company, with that of the other passengers; for my wife continued the whole day in a state of dozing, and my other females, whose sickness did not abate by the rolling of the ship at anchor, seemed more inclined to empty their stomachs than to fill them. Thus I passed the whole day (except about an hour at dinner) by myself, and the evening concluded with the captain as the preceding one had done; one comfortable piece of news he communicated to me, which was, that he had no doubt of a prosperous wind in the morning; but as he did not divulge the reasons of this confidence, and as I saw none myself besides the wind being directly opposite, my faith in this prophecy was not strong enough to build any great hopes upon.

Thursday, July 4.—This morning, however, the captain seemed resolved to fulfill his own predictions, whether the wind would or no; he accordingly weighed anchor, and, taking the advantage of the tide when the wind was not very boisterous, he hoisted his sails; and, as if his power had been no less absolute over Aeolus than it was over Neptune, he forced the wind to blow him on in its own despite.

But as all men who have ever been at sea well know how weak such attempts are, and want no authorities of Scripture to prove that the most absolute power of a captain of a ship is very contemptible in the wind's eye, so did it befall our noble commander, who, having struggled with the wind three or four hours, was obliged to give over, and lost in a few minutes all that he had been so long a-gaining; in short, we returned to our former station, and once more cast anchor in the neighborhood of Deal.

Here, though we lay near the shore, that we might promise ourselves all the emolument which could be derived from it, we found ourselves deceived; and that we might with as much conveniency be out of the sight of land; for, except when the captain launched forth his own boat, which he did always with great reluctance, we were incapable of procuring anything from Deal, but at a price too exorbitant, and beyond the reach even of modern luxury—the fare of a boat from Deal, which lay at two miles' distance, being at least three half-crowns, and, if we had been in any distress for it, as many half-guineas; for these good people consider the sea as a large common appendant to their manor; in which when they find any of their fellow-creatures impounded, they conclude that they have a full right of making them pay at their own discretion for their deliverance: to say the truth, whether it be that men who live on the sea-shore are of an amphibious kind, and do not entirely partake of human nature, or whatever else may be the reason, they are so far from taking any share in the distresses of mankind, or of being moved with any compassion for them, that they look upon them as blessings showered down from above, and which the more they improve to their own use, the greater is their gratitude and piety. Thus at Gravesend a sculler requires a shilling for going less way than he would row in London for threepence; and at Deal a boat often brings more profit in a day than it can produce in London in a week, or perhaps in a month; in both places the owner of the boat founds his demand on the necessity and distress of one who stands more or less in absolute want of his assistance, and with the urgency of these always rises in the exorbitancy of his demand, without ever considering that, from these very circumstances, the power or ease of gratifying such demand is in like proportion lessened. Now, as I am unwilling that some conclusions, which may be, I am aware, too justly drawn from these observations, should be imputed to human nature in general, I have endeavored to account for them in a way more consistent with the goodness and dignity of that nature. However it be, it seems a little to reflect on the governors of such monsters that they do not take some means to restrain these impositions, and prevent them from triumphing any longer in the miseries of those who are, in many circumstances at least, their fellow-creatures, and considering the distresses of a wretched seaman, from his being wrecked to his being barely windbound, as a blessing sent among them from above, and calling it by that blasphemous name.

Friday, July 5.—This day I sent a servant on board a man-of-war that was stationed here, with my compliments to the captain, to represent to him the distress of the ladies, and to desire the favor of his long-boat to conduct us to Dover, at about seven miles' distance; and at the same time presumed to make use of a great lady's name, the wife of the first lord commissioner of the admiralty, who would, I told him, be pleased with any kindness shown by him towards us in our miserable condition. And this I am convinced was true, from the humanity of the lady, though she was entirely unknown to me.

The captain returned a verbal answer to a long letter acquainting me that what I desired could not be complied with, it being a favor not in his power to grant. This might be, and I suppose was, true; but it is as true that, if he was able to write, and had pen, ink, and paper on board, he might have sent a written answer, and that it was the part of a gentleman so to have done; but this is a character seldom maintained on the watery element, especially by those who exercise any power on it. Every commander of a vessel here seems to think himself entirely free from all those rules of decency and civility which direct and restrain the conduct of the members of a society on shore; and each, claiming absolute dominion in his little wooden world, rules by his own laws and his own discretion. I do not, indeed, know so pregnant an instance of the dangerous consequences of absolute power, and its aptness to intoxicate the mind, as that of those petty tyrants, who become such in a moment, from very well-disposed and social members of that communion in which they affect no superiority, but live in an orderly state of legal subjection with their fellow-citizens.

Saturday, July 6.—This morning our commander, declaring he was sure the wind would change, took the advantage of an ebbing tide, and weighed his anchor. His assurance, however, had the same completion, and his endeavors the same success, with his formal trial; and he was soon obliged to return once more to his old quarters. Just before we let go our anchor, a small sloop, rather than submit to yield us an inch of way, ran foul of our ship, and carried off her bowsprit. This obstinate frolic would have cost those aboard the sloop very dear, if our steersman had not been too generous to exert his superiority, the certain consequence of which would have been the immediate sinking of the other. This contention of the inferior with a might capable of crushing it in an instant may seem to argue no small share of folly or madness, as well as of impudence; but I am convinced there is very little danger in it: contempt is a port to which the pride of man submits to fly with reluctance, but those who are within it are always in a place of the most assured security; for whosoever throws away his sword prefers, indeed, a less honorable but much safer means of avoiding danger than he who defends himself with it. And here we shall offer another distinction, of the truth of which much reading and experience have well convinced us, that as in the most absolute governments there is a regular progression of slavery downwards, from the top to the bottom, the mischief of which is seldom felt with any great force and bitterness but by the next immediate degree; so in the most dissolute and anarchical states there is as regular an ascent of what is called rank or condition, which is always laying hold of the head of him who is advanced but one step higher on the ladder, who might, if he did not too much despise such efforts, kick his pursuer headlong to the bottom. We will conclude this digression with one general and short observation, which will, perhaps, set the whole matter in a clearer light than the longest and most labored harangue. Whereas envy of all things most exposes us to danger from others, so contempt of all things best secures us from them. And thus, while the dung-cart and the sloop are always meditating mischief against the coach and the ship, and throwing themselves designedly in their way, the latter consider only their own security, and are not ashamed to break the road and let the other pass by them.

Monday, July 8.—Having passed our Sunday without anything remarkable, unless the catching a great number of whitings in the afternoon may be thought so, we now set sail on Monday at six o'clock, with a little variation of wind; but this was so very little, and the breeze itself so small, but the tide was our best and indeed almost our only friend. This conducted us along the short remainder of the Kentish shore. Here we passed that cliff of Dover which makes so tremendous a figure in Shakespeare, and which whoever reads without being giddy, must, according to Mr. Addison's observation, have either a very good head or a very bad, one; but which, whoever contracts any such ideas from the sight of, must have at least a poetic if not a Shakesperian genius. In truth, mountains, rivers, heroes, and gods owe great part of their existence to the poets; and Greece and Italy do so plentifully abound in the former, because they furnish so glorious a number of the latter; who, while they bestowed immortality on every little hillock and blind stream, left the noblest rivers and mountains in the world to share the same obscurity with the eastern and western poets, in which they are celebrated. This evening we beat the sea of Sussex in sight of Dungeness, with much more pleasure than progress; for the weather was almost a perfect calm, and the moon, which was almost at the full, scarce suffered a single cloud to veil her from our sight.

Tuesday, Wednesday, July 9, 10.—These two days we had much the same fine weather, and made much the same way; but in the evening of the latter day a pretty fresh gale sprung up at N.N.W., which brought us by the morning in sight of the Isle of Wight.

Thursday, July 11.—This gale continued till towards noon; when the east end of the island bore but little ahead of us. The captain swaggered and declared he would keep the sea; but the wind got the better of him, so that about three he gave up the victory, and making a sudden tack stood in for the shore, passed by Spithead and Portsmouth, and came to an anchor at a place called Ryde on the island.

A most tragical incident fell out this day at sea. While the ship was under sail, but making as will appear no great way, a kitten, one of four of the feline inhabitants of the cabin, fell from the window into the water: an alarm was immediately given to the captain, who was then upon deck, and received it with the utmost concern and many bitter oaths. He immediately gave orders to the steersman in favor of the poor thing, as he called it; the sails were instantly slackened, and all hands, as the phrase is, employed to recover the poor animal. I was, I own, extremely surprised at all this; less indeed at the captain's extreme tenderness than at his conceiving any possibility of success; for if puss had had nine thousand instead of nine lives, I concluded they had been all lost. The boatswain, however, had more sanguine hopes, for, having stripped himself of his jacket, breeches, and shirt, he leaped boldly into the water, and to my great astonishment in a few minutes returned to the ship, bearing the motionless animal in his mouth. Nor was this, I observed, a matter of such great difficulty as it appeared to my ignorance, and possibly may seem to that of my fresh-water reader. The kitten was now exposed to air and sun on the deck, where its life, of which it retained no symptoms, was despaired of by all.

The captain's humanity, if I may so call it, did not so totally destroy his philosophy as to make him yield himself up to affliction on this melancholy occasion. Having felt his loss like a man, he resolved to show he could bear it like one; and, having declared he had rather have lost a cask of rum or brandy, betook himself to threshing at backgammon with the Portuguese friar, in which innocent amusement they had passed about two-thirds of their time.

But as I have, perhaps, a little too wantonly endeavored to raise the tender passions of my readers in this narrative, I should think myself unpardonable if I concluded it without giving them the satisfaction of hearing that the kitten at last recovered, to the great joy of the good captain, but to the great disappointment of some of the sailors, who asserted that the drowning a cat was the very surest way of raising a favorable wind; a supposition of which, though we have heard several plausible accounts, we will not presume to assign the true original reason.

Friday, July 12.—This day our ladies went ashore at Ryde, and drank their afternoon tea at an ale-house there with great satisfaction: here they were regaled with fresh cream, to which they had been strangers since they left the Downs.

Saturday, July 13.—The wind seeming likely to continue in the same corner where it had been almost constantly for two months together, I was persuaded by my wife to go ashore and stay at Ryde till we sailed. I approved the motion much; for though I am a great lover of the sea, I now fancied there was more pleasure in breathing the fresh air of the land; but how to get thither was the question; for, being really that dead luggage which I considered all passengers to be in the beginning of this narrative, and incapable of any bodily motion without external impulse, it was in vain to leave the ship, or to determine to do it, without the assistance of others. In one instance, perhaps, the living, luggage is more difficult to be moved or removed than an equal or much superior weight of dead matter; which, if of the brittle kind, may indeed be liable to be broken through negligence; but this, by proper care, may be almost certainly prevented; whereas the fractures to which the living lumps are exposed are sometimes by no caution avoidable, and often by no art to be amended.

I was deliberating on the means of conveyance, not so much out of the ship to the boat as out of a little tottering boat to the land; a matter which, as I had already experienced in the Thames, was not extremely easy, when to be performed by any other limbs than your own. Whilst I weighed all that could suggest itself on this head, without strictly examining the merit of the several schemes which were advanced by the captain and sailors, and, indeed, giving no very deep attention even to my wife, who, as well as her friend and my daughter, were exerting their tender concern for my ease and safety, Fortune, for I am convinced she had a hand in it, sent me a present of a buck; a present welcome enough of itself, but more welcome on account of the vessel in which it came, being a large hoy, which in some places would pass for a ship, and many people would go some miles to see the sight.

I was pretty easily conveyed on board this hoy; but to get from hence to the shore was not so easy a task; for, however strange it may appear, the water itself did not extend so far; an instance which seems to explain those lines of Ovid,

Omnia pontus erant, deerant quoque littora ponto,

in a less tautological sense than hath generally been imputed to them.

In fact, between the sea and the shore there was, at low water, an impassable gulf, if I may so call it, of deep mud, which could neither be traversed by walking nor swimming; so that for near one half of the twenty-four hours Ryde was inaccessible by friend or foe. But as the magistrates of this place seemed more to desire the company of the former than to fear that of the latter, they had begun to make a small causeway to the low-water mark, so that foot passengers might land whenever they pleased; but as this work was of a public kind, and would have cost a large sum of money, at least ten pounds, and the magistrates, that is to say, the churchwardens, the overseers, constable, and tithingman, and the principal inhabitants, had every one of them some separate scheme of private interest to advance at the expense of the public, they fell out among themselves; and, after having thrown away one half of the requisite sum, resolved at least to save the other half, and rather be contented to sit down losers themselves than to enjoy any benefit which might bring in a greater profit to another. Thus that unanimity which is so necessary in all public affairs became wanting, and every man, from the fear of being a bubble to another, was, in reality, a bubble to himself.

However, as there is scarce any difficulty to which the strength of men, assisted with the cunning of art, is not equal, I was at last hoisted into a small boat, and being rowed pretty near the shore, was taken up by two sailors, who waded with me through the mud, and placed me in a chair on the land, whence they afterwards conveyed me a quarter of a mile farther, and brought me to a house which seemed to bid the fairest for hospitality of any in Ryde.

We brought with us our provisions from the ship, so that we wanted nothing but a fire to dress our dinner, and a room in which we might eat it. In neither of these had we any reason to apprehend a disappointment, our dinner consisting only of beans and bacon; and the worst apartment in his majesty's dominions, either at home or abroad, being fully sufficient to answer our present ideas of delicacy.

Unluckily, however, we were disappointed in both; for when we arrived about four at our inn, exulting in the hopes of immediately seeing our beans smoking on the table, we had the mortification of seeing them on the table indeed, but without that circumstance which would have made the sight agreeable, being in the same state in which we had dispatched them from our ship. In excuse for this delay, though we had exceeded, almost purposely, the time appointed, and our provision had arrived three hours before, the mistress of the house acquainted us that it was not for want of time to dress them that they were not ready, but for fear of their being cold or over-done before we should come; which she assured us was much worse than waiting a few minutes for our dinner; an observation so very just, that it is impossible to find any objection in it; but, indeed, it was not altogether so proper at this time, for we had given the most absolute orders to have them ready at four, and had been ourselves, not without much care and difficulty, most exactly punctual in keeping to the very minute of our appointment. But tradesmen, inn-keepers, and servants, never care to indulge us in matters contrary to our true interest, which they always know better than ourselves; nor can any bribes corrupt them to go out of their way while they are consulting our good in our own despite.

Our disappointment in the other particular, in defiance of our humility, as it was more extraordinary, was more provoking. In short, Mrs. Francis (for that was the name of the good woman of the house) no sooner received the news of our intended arrival than she considered more the gentility than the humanity of her guests, and applied herself not to that which kindles but to that which extinguishes fire, and, forgetting to put on her pot, fell to washing her house.

As the messenger who had brought my venison was impatient to be dispatched, I ordered it to be brought and laid on the table in the room where I was seated; and the table not being large enough, one side, and that a very bloody one, was laid on the brick floor. I then ordered Mrs. Francis to be called in, in order to give her instructions concerning it; in particular, what I would have roasted and what baked; concluding that she would be highly pleased with the prospect of so much money being spent in her house as she might have now reason to expect, if the wind continued only a few days longer to blow from the same points whence it had blown for several weeks past.

I soon saw good cause, I must confess, to despise my own sagacity. Mrs. Francis, having received her orders, without making any answer, snatched the side from the floor, which remained stained with blood, and, bidding a servant to take up that on the table, left the room with no pleasant countenance, muttering to herself that, "had she known the litter which was to have been made, she would not have taken such pains to wash her house that morning. If this was gentility, much good may it do such gentlefolks; for her part she had no notion of it." From these murmurs I received two hints. The one, that it was not from a mistake of our inclination that the good woman had starved us, but from wisely consulting her own dignity, or rather perhaps her vanity, to which our hunger was offered up as a sacrifice. The other, that I was now sitting in a damp room, a circumstance, though it had hitherto escaped my notice from the color of the bricks, which was by no means to be neglected in a valetudinary state.

My wife, who, besides discharging excellently well her own and all the tender offices becoming the female character; who, besides being a faithful friend, an amiable companion, and a tender nurse, could likewise supply the wants of a decrepit husband, and occasionally perform his part, had, before this, discovered the immoderate attention to neatness in Mrs. Francis, and provided against its ill consequences. She had found, though not under the same roof, a very snug apartment belonging to Mr. Francis, and which had escaped the mop by his wife's being satisfied it could not possibly be visited by gentle-folks. This was a dry, warm, oaken-floored barn, lined on both sides with wheaten straw, and opening at one end into a green field and a beautiful prospect. Here, without hesitation, she ordered the cloth to be laid, and came hastily to snatch me from worse perils by water than the common dangers of the sea.

Mrs. Francis, who could not trust her own ears, or could not believe a footman in so extraordinary a phenomenon, followed my wife, and asked her if she had indeed ordered the cloth to be laid in the barn? She answered in the affirmative; upon which Mrs. Francis declared she would not dispute her pleasure, but it was the first time she believed that quality had ever preferred a barn to a house. She showed at the same time the most pregnant marks of contempt, and again lamented the labor she had undergone, through her ignorance of the absurd taste of her guests.

At length we were seated in one of the most pleasant spots I believe in the kingdom, and were regaled with our beans and bacon, in which there was nothing deficient but the quantity. This defect was however so deplorable that we had consumed our whole dish before we had visibly lessened our hunger. We now waited with impatience the arrival of our second course, which necessity, and not luxury, had dictated. This was a joint of mutton which Mrs. Francis had been ordered to provide; but when, being tired with expectation, we ordered our servants TO SEE FOR SOMETHING ELSE, we were informed that there was nothing else; on which Mrs. Francis, being summoned, declared there was no such thing as mutton to be had at Ryde. When I expressed some astonishment at their having no butcher in a village so situated, she answered they had a very good one, and one that killed all sorts of meat in season, beef two or three times a year, and mutton the whole year round; but that, it being then beans and peas time, he killed no meat, by reason he was not sure of selling it. This she had not thought worthy of communication, any more than that there lived a fisherman at next door, who was then provided with plenty of soles, and whitings, and lobsters, far superior to those which adorn a city feast. This discovery being made by accident, we completed the best, the pleasantest, and the merriest meal, with more appetite, more real solid luxury, and more festivity, than was ever seen in an entertainment at White's.

It may be wondered at, perhaps, that Mrs. Francis should be so negligent of providing for her guests, as she may seem to be thus inattentive to her own interest; but this was not the case; for, having clapped a poll-tax on our heads at our arrival, and determined at what price to discharge our bodies from her house, the less she suffered any other to share in the levy the clearer it came into her own pocket; and that it was better to get twelve pence in a shilling than ten pence, which latter would be the case if she afforded us fish at any rate.

Thus we passed a most agreeable day owing to good appetites and good humor; two hearty feeders which will devour with satisfaction whatever food you place before them; whereas, without these, the elegance of St. James's, the charde, the perigord-pie, or the ortolan, the venison, the turtle, or the custard, may titillate the throat, but will never convey happiness to the heart or cheerfulness to the countenance.

As the wind appeared still immovable, my wife proposed my lying on shore. I presently agreed, though in defiance of an act of parliament, by which persons wandering abroad and lodging in ale-houses are decreed to be rogues and vagabonds; and this too after having been very singularly officious in putting that law in execution. My wife, having reconnoitered the house, reported that there was one room in which were two beds. It was concluded, therefore, that she and Harriot should occupy one and myself take possession of the other. She added likewise an ingenious recommendation of this room to one who had so long been in a cabin, which it exactly resembled, as it was sunk down with age on one side, and was in the form of a ship with gunwales too.

For my own part, I make little doubt but this apartment was an ancient temple, built with the materials of a wreck, and probably dedicated to Neptune in honor of THE BLESSING sent by him to the inhabitants; such blessings having in all ages been very common to them. The timber employed in it confirms this opinion, being such as is seldom used by ally but ship-builders. I do not find indeed any mention of this matter in Hearn; but perhaps its antiquity was too modern to deserve his notice. Certain it is that this island of Wight was not an early convert to Christianity; nay, there is some reason to doubt whether it was ever entirely converted. But I have only time to touch slightly on things of this kind, which, luckily for us, we have a society whose peculiar profession it is to discuss and develop.

Sunday, July 19.—This morning early I summoned Mrs. Francis, in order to pay her the preceding day's account. As I could recollect only two or three articles I thought there was no necessity of pen and ink. In a single instance only we had exceeded what the law allows gratis to a foot-soldier on his march, viz., vinegar, salt, etc., and dressing his meat. I found, however, I was mistaken in my calculation; for when the good woman attended with her bill it contained as follows: —

	L.	s.	d.
Bread and beer	0	2	4
Wind	0	2	0
Rum	0	2	0
Dressing dinner	0	3	0
Tea	0	1	6
Firing	0	1	0
Lodging	0	1	6
Servants' lodging	0	0	6
	L 0	13	10

Now that five people and two servants should live a day and night at a public-house for so small a sum will appear incredible to any person in London above the degree of a chimney-sweeper; but more astonishing will it seem that these people should remain so long at such a house without tasting any other delicacy than bread, small beer, a teacupful of milk called cream, a glass of rum converted into punch by their own materials, and one bottle of wind, of which we only tasted a single glass though possibly, indeed, our servants drank the remainder of the bottle.

This wind is a liquor of English manufacture, and its flavor is thought very delicious by the generality of the English, who drink it in great quantities. Every seventh year is thought to produce as much as the other six. It is then drank so plentifully that the whole nation are in a manner intoxicated by it; and consequently very little business is carried on at that season. It resembles in color the red wine which is imported from Portugal, as it doth in its intoxicating quality; hence, and from this agreement in the orthography, the one is often confounded with the other, though both are seldom esteemed by the same person. It is to be had in every parish of the kingdom, and a pretty large quantity is consumed in the metropolis, where several taverns are set apart solely for the vendition of this liquor, the masters never dealing in any other. The disagreement in our computation produced some small remonstrance to Mrs. Francis on my side; but this received an immediate answer: "She scorned to overcharge gentlemen; her house had been always frequented by the very best gentry of the island; and she had never had a bill found fault with in her life, though she had lived upwards of forty years in the house, and within that time the greatest gentry in Hampshire had been at it; and that lawyer Willis never went to any other when he came to those parts. That for her part she did not get her livelihood by travelers, who were gone and away, and she never expected to see them more, but that her neighbors might come again; wherefore, to be sure, they had the only right to complain."

She was proceeding thus, and from her volubility of tongue seemed likely to stretch the discourse to an immoderate length, when I suddenly cut all short by paying the bill.

This morning our ladies went to church, more, I fear, from curiosity than religion; they were attended by the captain in a most military attire, with his cockade in his hat and his sword by his side. So unusual an appearance in this little chapel drew the attention of all present, and probably disconcerted the women, who were in dishabille, and wished themselves dressed, for the sake of the curate, who was the greatest of their beholders. While I was left alone I received a visit from Mr. Francis himself, who was much more considerable as a farmer than as an inn-holder. Indeed, he left the latter entirely to the care of his wife, and he acted wisely, I believe, in so doing. As nothing more remarkable passed on this day I will close it with the account of these two characters, as far as a few days' residence could inform me of them. If they should appear as new to the reader as they did to me, he will not be displeased at finding them here. This amiable couple seemed to border hard on their grand climacteric; nor indeed were they shy of owning enough to fix their ages within a year or two of that time. They appeared to be rather proud of having employed their time well than ashamed of having lived so long; the only reason which I could ever assign why some fine ladies, and fine gentlemen too, should desire to be thought younger than they really are by the contemporaries of their grandchildren. Some, indeed, who too hastily credit appearances, might doubt whether they had made so good a use of their time as I would insinuate, since there was no appearance of anything but poverty, want, and wretchedness, about their house; nor could they produce anything to a customer in exchange for his money but a few bottles of wind, and spirituous liquors, and some very bad ale, to drink; with rusty bacon and worse cheese to eat. But then it should be considered, on the other side, that whatever they received was almost as entirely clear profit as the blessing of a wreck itself; such an inn being the very reverse of a coffee-house; for here you can neither sit for nothing nor have anything for your money.

Again, as many marks of want abounded everywhere, so were the marks of antiquity visible. Scarce anything was to be seen which had not some scar upon it, made by the hand of Time; not an utensil, it was manifest, had been purchased within a dozen years last past; so that whatever money had come into the house during that period at least must have remained in it, unless it had been sent abroad for food, or other perishable commodities; but these were supplied by a small portion of the fruits of the farm, in which the farmer allowed he had a very good bargain. In fact, it is inconceivable what sums may be collected by starving only, and how easy it is for a man to die rich if he will but be contented to live miserable.

Nor is there in this kind of starving anything so terrible as some apprehend. It neither wastes a man's flesh nor robs him of his cheerfulness. The famous Cornaro's case well proves the contrary; and so did farmer Francis, who was of a round stature, had a plump, round face, with a kind of smile on it, and seemed to borrow an air of wretchedness rather from his coat's age than from his own.

The truth is, there is a certain diet which emaciates men more than any possible degree of abstinence; though I do not remember to have seen any caution against it, either in Cheney, Arbuthnot, or in any other modern writer or regimen.

Nay, the very name is not, I believe, in the learned Dr. James's Dictionary; all which is the more extraordinary as it is a very common food in this kingdom, and the college themselves were not long since very liberally entertained with it by the present attorney and other eminent lawyers in Lincoln's-inn-hall, and were all made horribly sick by it.

But though it should not be found among our English physical writers, we may be assured of meeting with it among the Greeks; for nothing considerable in nature escapes their notice, though many things considerable in them, it is to be feared, have escaped the notice of their readers. The Greeks, then, to all such as feed too voraciously on this diet, give the name of HEAUTOFAGI, which our physicians will, I suppose, translate MEN THAT EAT THEMSELVES.

As nothing is so destructive to the body as this kind of food, so nothing is so plentiful and cheap; but it was perhaps the only cheap thing the farmer disliked. Probably living much on fish might produce this disgust; for Diodorus Siculus attributes the same aversion in a people of Ethiopia to the same cause; he calls them the fish-eaters, and asserts that they cannot be brought to eat a single meal with the Heautofagi by any persuasion, threat, or violence whatever, not even though they should kill their children before their faces.

What hath puzzled our physicians, and prevented them from setting this matter in the clearest light, is possibly one simple mistake, arising from a very excusable ignorance; that the passions of men are capable of swallowing food as well as their appetites; that the former, in feeding, resemble the state of those animals who chew the cud; and therefore, such men, in some sense, may be said to prey on themselves, and as it were to devour their own entrails. And hence ensues a meager aspect and thin habit of body, as surely as from what is called a consumption. Our farmer was one of these. He had no more passion than an Ichthuofagus or Ethiopian fisher. He wished not for anything, thought not of anything; indeed, he scarce did anything or said anything. Here I cannot be understood strictly;

for then I must describe a nonentity, whereas I would rob him of nothing but that free agency which is the cause of all the corruption and of all the misery of human nature. No man, indeed, ever did more than the farmer, for he was an absolute slave to labor all the week; but in truth, as my sagacious reader must have at first apprehended, when I said he resigned the care of the house to his wife, I meant more than I then expressed, even the house and all that belonged to it; for he was really a farmer only under the direction of his wife. In a word, so composed, so serene, so placid a countenance, I never saw; and he satisfied himself by answering to every question he was asked, "I don't know anything about it, sir; I leaves all that to my wife."

Now, as a couple of this kind would, like two vessels of oil, have made no composition in life, and for want of all savor must have palled every taste; nature or fortune, or both of them, took care to provide a proper quantity of acid in the materials that formed the wife, and to render her a perfect helpmate for so tranquil a husband. She abounded in whatsoever he was defective; that is to say, in almost everything. She was indeed as vinegar to oil, or a brisk wind to a standing-pool, and preserved all from stagnation and corruption.

Quin the player, on taking a nice and severe survey of a fellow-comedian, burst forth into this exclamation:—"If that fellow be not a rogue, God Almighty doth not write a legible hand."

Whether he guessed right or no is not worth my while to examine; certain it is that the latter, having wrought his features into a proper harmony to become the characters of Iago, Shylock, and others of the same cast, gave us a semblance of truth to the observation that was sufficient to confirm the wit of it. Indeed, we may remark, in favor of the physiognomist, though the law has made him a rogue and vagabond, that Nature is seldom curious in her works within, without employing some little pains on the outside; and this more particularly in mischievous characters, in forming which, as Mr. Derham observes, in venomous insects, as the sting or saw of a wasp, she is sometimes wonderfully industrious. Now, when she hath thus completely armed our hero to carry on a war with man, she never fails of furnishing that innocent lambkin with some means of knowing his enemy, and foreseeing his designs. Thus she hath been observed to act in the case of a rattlesnake, which never meditates a human prey without giving warning of his approach.

This observation will, I am convinced, hold most true, if applied to the most venomous individuals of human insects. A tyrant, a trickster, and a bully, generally wear the marks of their several dispositions in their countenances; so do the vixen, the shrew, the scold, and all other females of the like kind. But, perhaps, nature hath never afforded a stronger example of all this than in the case of Mrs. Francis. She was a short, squat woman; her head was closely joined to her shoulders, where it was fixed somewhat awry; every feature of her countenance was sharp and pointed; her face was furrowed with the smallpox; and her complexion, which seemed to be able to turn milk to curds, not a little resembled in color such milk as had already undergone that operation. She appeared, indeed, to have many symptoms of a deep jaundice in her look; but the strength and firmness of her voice overbalanced them all; the tone of this was a sharp treble at a distance, for I seldom heard it on the same floor, but was usually waked with it in the morning, and entertained with it almost continually through the whole day.

Though vocal be usually put in opposition to instrumental music, I question whether this might not be thought to partake of the nature of both; for she played on two instruments, which she seemed to keep for no other use from morning till night; these were two maids, or rather scolding-stocks, who, I suppose, by some means or other, earned their board, and she gave them their lodging gratis, or for no other service than to keep her lungs in constant exercise.

She differed, as I have said, in every particular from her husband; but very remarkably in this, that, as it was impossible to displease him, so it was as impossible to please her; and as no art could remove a smile from his countenance, so could no art carry it into hers. If her bills were remonstrated against she was offended with the tacit censure of her fair-dealing; if they were not, she seemed to regard it as a tacit sarcasm on her folly, which might have set down larger prices with the same success. On this lather hint she did indeed improve, for she daily raised some of her articles. A pennyworth of fire was to-day rated at a shilling, to-morrow at eighteen-pence; and if she dressed us two dishes for two shillings on the Saturday, we paid half-a-crown for the cookery of one on the Sunday; and, whenever she was paid, she never left the room without lamenting the small amount of her bill, saying, "she knew not how it was that others got their money by gentle-folks, but for her part she had not the art of it." When she was asked why she complained, when she was paid all she demanded, she answered, "she could not deny that, nor did she know she had omitted anything; but that it was but a poor bill for gentle-folks to pay." I accounted for all this by her having heard, that it is a maxim with the principal inn-holders on the continent, to levy considerable sums on their guests, who travel with many horses and servants, though such guests should eat little or nothing in their houses; the method being, I believe, in such cases, to lay a capitation on the horses, and not on their masters. But she did not consider that in most of these inns a very great degree of hunger, without any degree of delicacy, may be satisfied; and that in all such inns there is some appearance, at least, of provision, as well as of a man-cook to dress it, one of the hostlers being always furnished with a cook's cap, waistcoat, and apron, ready to attend gentlemen and ladies on their summons; that the case therefore of such inns differed from hers, where there was nothing to eat or to drink, and in reality no house to inhabit, no chair to sit upon, nor any bed to lie in; that one third or fourth part therefore of the levy imposed at inns was, in truth, a higher tax than the whole was when laid on in the other, where, in order to raise a small sum, a man is obliged to submit to pay as many various ways for the same thing as he doth to the government for the light which enters through his own window into his own house, from his own estate; such are the articles of bread and beer, firing, eating and dressing dinner.

The foregoing is a very imperfect sketch of this extraordinary couple; for everything is here lowered instead of being heightened. Those who would see them set forth in more lively colors, and with the proper ornaments, may read the descriptions of the Furies in some of the classical poets, or of the Stoic philosophers in the works of Lucian.

Monday, July 20.—This day nothing remarkable passed; Mrs. Francis levied a tax of fourteen shillings for the Sunday. We regaled ourselves at dinner with venison and good claret of our own; and in the afternoon, the women, attended by the captain, walked to see a delightful scene two miles distant, with the beauties of which they declared themselves most highly charmed at their return, as well as with the goodness of the lady of the mansion, who had slipped out of the way that my wife and their company might refresh themselves with the flowers and fruits with which her garden abounded.

Tuesday, July 21.—This day, having paid our taxes of yesterday, we were permitted to regale ourselves with more venison. Some of this we would willingly have exchanged for mutton; but no such flesh was to be had nearer than Portsmouth, from whence it would have cost more to convey a joint to us than the freight of a Portugal ham from Lisbon to London amounts to; for though the water-carriage be somewhat cheaper here than at Deal, yet can you find no waterman who will go on board his boat, unless by two or three hours' rowing he can get drunk for the residue of the week.

And here I have an opportunity, which possibly may not offer again, of publishing some observations on that political economy of this nation, which, as it concerns only the regulation of the mob, is below the notice of our great men; though on the due regulation of this order depend many emoluments, which the great men themselves, or at least many who tread close on their heels, may enjoy, as well as some dangers which may some time or other arise from introducing a pure state of anarchy among them. I will represent the case, as it appears to me, very fairly and impartially between the mob and their betters. The whole mischief which infects this part of our economy arises from the vague and uncertain use of a word called liberty, of which, as scarce any two men with whom I have ever conversed seem to have one and the same idea, I am inclined to doubt whether there be any simple universal notion represented by this word, or whether it conveys any clearer or more determinate idea than some of those old Punic compositions of syllables preserved in one of the comedies of Plautus, but at present, as I conceive, not supposed to be understood by any one.

By liberty, however, I apprehend, is commonly understood the power of doing what we please; not absolutely, for then it would be inconsistent with law, by whose control the liberty of the freest people, except only the Hottentots and wild Indians, must always be restrained.

But, indeed, however largely we extend, or however moderately we confine, the sense of the word, no politician will, I presume, contend that it is to pervade in an equal degree, and be, with the same extent, enjoyed by, every member of society; no such polity having been ever found, unless among those vile people just before commemorated. Among the Greeks and Romans the servile and free conditions were opposed to each other; and no man who had the misfortune to be enrolled under the former could lay any claim to liberty till the right was conveyed to him by that master whose slave he was, either by the means of conquest, of purchase, or of birth.

This was the state of all the free nations in the world; and this, till very lately, was understood to be the case of our own.

I will not indeed say this is the case at present, the lowest class of our people having shaken off all the shackles of their superiors, and become not only as free, but even freer, than most of their superiors. I believe it cannot be doubted, though perhaps we have no recent instance of it, that the personal attendance of every man who hath three hundred pounds per annum, in parliament, is indispensably his duty; and that, if the citizens and burgesses of any city or borough shall choose such a one, however reluctant he appear, he may be obliged to attend, and be forcibly brought to his duty by the sergeant-at-arms.

Again, there are numbers of subordinate offices, some of which are of burden, and others of expense, in the civil government—all of which persons who are qualified are liable to have imposed on them, may be obliged to undertake and properly execute, notwithstanding any bodily labor, or even danger, to which they may subject themselves, under the penalty of fines and imprisonment; nay, and what may appear somewhat hard, may be compelled to satisfy the losses which are eventually incident, to that of sheriff in particular, out of their own private fortunes; and though this should prove the ruin of a family, yet the public, to whom the price is due, incurs no debt or obligation to preserve its officer harmless, let his innocence appear ever so clearly. I purposely omit the mention of those military or military duties which our old constitution laid upon its greatest members. These might, indeed, supply their posts with some other able-bodied men; but if no such could have been found, the obligation nevertheless remained, and they were compellable to serve in their own proper persons. The only one, therefore, who is possessed of absolute liberty is the lowest member of the society, who, if he prefers hunger, or the wild product of the fields, hedges, lanes, and rivers, with the indulgence of ease and laziness, to a food a little more delicate, but purchased at the expense of labor, may lay himself under a shade; nor can be forced to take the other alternative from that which he hath, I will not affirm whether wisely or foolishly, chosen.

Here I may, perhaps, be reminded of the last Vagrant Act, where all such persons are compellable to work for the usual and accustomed wages allowed in the place; but this is a clause little known to the justices of the peace, and least likely to be executed by those who do know it, as they know likewise that it is formed on the ancient power of the justices to fix and settle these wages every year, making proper allowances for the scarcity and plenty of the times, the cheapness and dearness of the place; and that THE USUAL AND ACCUSTOMED WAGES are words without any force or meaning, when there are no such; but every man spunges and raps whatever he can get; and will haggle as long and struggle as hard to cheat his employer of twopence in a day's labor as an honest tradesman will to cheat his customers of the same sum in a yard of cloth or silk.

It is a great pity then that this power, or rather this practice, was not revived; but, this having been so long omitted that it is become obsolete, will be best done by a new law, in which this power, as well as the consequent power of forcing the poor to labor at a moderate and reasonable rate, should be well considered and their execution facilitated; for gentlemen who give their time and labor gratis, and even voluntarily, to the public, have a right to expect that all their business be made as easy as possible; and to enact laws without doing this is to fill our statute-books, much too full already, still fuller with dead letter, of no use but to the printer of the acts of parliament. That the evil which I have here pointed at is of itself worth redressing, is, I apprehend, no subject of dispute; for why should any persons in distress be deprived of the assistance of their fellow-subjects, when they are willing amply to reward them for their labor? or, why should the lowest of the people be permitted to exact ten times the value of their work? For those exactions increase with the degrees of necessity in their object, insomuch that on the former side many are horribly imposed upon, and that often in no trifling matters. I was very well assured that at Deal no less than ten guineas was required, and paid by the supercargo of an Indiaman, for carrying him on board two miles from the shore when she was just ready to sail; so that his necessity, as his pillager well understood, was absolute. Again, many others, whose indignation will not submit to such plunder, are forced to refuse the assistance, though they are often great sufferers by so doing. On the latter side, the lowest of the people are encouraged in laziness and idleness; while they live by a twentieth part of the labor that ought to maintain them, which is diametrically opposite to the interest of the public; for that requires a great deal to be done, not to be paid, for a little. And moreover, they are confirmed in habits of exaction, and are taught to consider the distresses of their superiors as their own fair emolument. But enough of this matter, of which I at first intended only to convey a hint to those who are alone capable of applying the remedy, though they are the last to whom the notice of those evils would occur, without some such monitor as myself, who am forced to travel about the world in the form of a passenger. I cannot but say I heartily wish our governors would attentively consider this method of fixing the price of labor, and by that means of compelling the poor to work, since the due execution of such powers will, I apprehend, be found the true and only means of making them useful, and of advancing trade from its present visibly declining state to the height to which Sir William Petty, in his Political Arithmetic, thinks it capable of being carried.

In the afternoon the lady of the above-mentioned mansion called at our inn, and left her compliments to us with Mrs. Francis, with an assurance that while we continued wind-bound in that place, where she feared we could be but indifferently accommodated, we were extremely welcome to the use of anything which her garden or her house afforded. So polite a message convinced us, in spite of some arguments to the contrary, that we were not on the coast of Africa, or on some island where the few savage inhabitants have little of human in them besides their form. And here I mean nothing less than to derogate from the merit of this lady, who is not only extremely polite in her behavior to strangers of her own rank, but so extremely good and charitable to all her poor neighbors who stand in need of her assistance, that she hath the universal love and praises of all who live near her. But, in reality, how little doth the acquisition of so valuable a character, and the full indulgence of so worthy a disposition, cost those who possess it! Both are accomplished by the very offals which fall from a table moderately plentiful. That they are enjoyed therefore by so few arises truly from there being so few who have any such disposition to gratify, or who aim at any such character.

Wednesday, July 22.—This morning, after having been mulcted as usual, we dispatched a servant with proper acknowledgments of the lady's goodness; but confined our wants entirely to the productions of her garden. He soon returned, in company with the gardener, both richly laden with almost every particular which a garden at this most fruitful season of the year produces. While we were regaling ourselves with these, towards the close of our dinner, we received orders from our commander, who had dined that day with some inferior officers on board a man-of-war, to return instantly to the ship; for that the wind was become favorable and he should weigh that evening. These orders were soon followed by the captain himself, who was still in the utmost hurry, though the occasion of it had long since ceased; for the wind had, indeed, a little shifted that afternoon, but was before this very quietly set down in its old quarters.

This last was a lucky hit for me; for, as the captain, to whose orders we resolved to pay no obedience, unless delivered by himself, did not return till past six, so much time seemed requisite to put up the furniture of our bed-chamber or dining-room, for almost every article, even to some of the chairs, were either our own or the captain's property; so much more in conveying it as well as myself, as dead a luggage as any, to the shore, and thence to the ship, that the night threatened first to overtake us. A terrible circumstance to me, in my decayed condition; especially as very heavy showers of rain, attended with a high wind, continued to fall incessantly; the being carried through which two miles in the dark, in a wet and open boat, seemed little less than certain death. However, as my commander was absolute, his orders peremptory, and my obedience necessary, I resolved to avail myself of a philosophy which hath been of notable use to me in the latter part of my life, and which is contained in this hemistich of Virgil:—

——Superanda omnis fortuna ferendo est.

The meaning of which, if Virgil had any, I think I rightly understood, and rightly applied. As I was therefore to be entirely passive in my motion, I resolved to abandon myself to the conduct of those who were to carry me into a cart when it returned from unloading the goods.

But before this, the captain, perceiving what had happened in the clouds, and that the wind remained as much his enemy as ever, came upstairs to me with a reprieve till the morning. This was, I own, very agreeable news, and I little regretted the trouble of refurnishing my apartment, by sending back for the goods.

Mrs. Francis was not well pleased with this.

As she understood the reprieve to be only till the morning, she saw nothing but lodging to be possibly added, out of which she was to deduct fire and candle, and the remainder, she thought, would scarce pay her for her trouble. She exerted therefore all the ill-humor of which she was mistress, and did all she could to thwart and perplex everything during the whole evening.

Thursday, July 23.—Early in the morning the captain, who had remained on shore all night, came to visit us, and to press us to make haste on board. "I am resolved," says he, "not to lose a moment now the wind is coming about fair: for my own part, I never was surer of a wind in all my life." I use his very words; nor will I presume to interpret or comment upon them farther than by observing that they were spoke in the utmost hurry.

We promised to be ready as soon as breakfast was over, but this was not so soon as was expected; for, in removing our goods the evening before, the tea-chest was unhappily lost. Every place was immediately searched, and many where it was impossible for it to be; for this was a loss of much greater consequence than it may at first seem to many of my readers. Ladies and valetudinarians do not easily dispense with the use of this sovereign cordial in a single instance; but to undertake a long voyage, without any probability of being supplied with it the whole way, was above the reach of patience. And yet, dreadful as this calamity was, it seemed unavoidable. The whole town of Ryde could not supply a single leaf; for, as to what Mrs. Francis and the shop called by that name, it was not of Chinese growth. It did not indeed in the least resemble tea, either in smell or taste, or in any particular, unless in being a leaf; for it was in truth no other than a tobacco of the mundungus species. And as for the hopes of relief in any other port, they were not to be depended upon, for the captain had positively declared he was sure of a wind, and would let go his anchor no more till he arrived in the Tajo.

When a good deal of time had been spent, most of it indeed wasted on this occasion, a thought occurred which every one wondered at its not having presented itself the first moment. This was to apply to the good lady, who could not fail of pitying and relieving such distress. A messenger was immediately despatched with an account of our misfortune, till whose return we employed ourselves in preparatives for our departure, that we might have nothing to do but to swallow our breakfast when it arrived. The tea-chest, though of no less consequence to us than the military-chest to a general, was given up as lost, or rather as stolen, for though I would not, for the world, mention any particular name, it is certain we had suspicions, and all, I am afraid, fell on the same person.

The man returned from the worthy lady with much expedition, and brought with him a canister of tea, despatched with so true a generosity, as well as politeness, that if our voyage had been as long again we should have incurred no danger of being brought to a short allowance in this most important article. At the very same instant likewise arrived William the footman with our own tea-chest. It had been, indeed, left in the hoy, when the other goods were re-landed, as William, when he first heard it was missing, had suspected; and whence, had not the owner of the hoy been unluckily out of the way, he had retrieved it soon enough to have prevented our giving the lady an opportunity of displaying some part of her goodness. To search the hoy was, indeed, too natural a suggestion to have escaped any one, nor did it escape being mentioned by many of us; but we were dissuaded from it by my wife's maid, who perfectly well remembered she had left the chest in the bed-chamber; for that she had never given it out of her hand in her way to or from the hoy; but William perhaps knew the maid better, and best understood how far she was to be believed; for otherwise he would hardly of his own accord, after hearing her declaration, have hunted out the hoy-man, with much pains and difficulty. Thus ended this scene, which began with such appearance of distress, and ended with becoming the subject of mirth and laughter. Nothing now remained but to pay our taxes, which were indeed laid with inconceivable severity. Lodging was raised sixpence, fire in the same proportion, and even candles, which had hitherto escaped, were charged with a wantonness of imposition, from the beginning, and placed under the style of oversight. We were raised a whole pound, whereas we had only burned ten, in five nights, and the pound consisted of twenty-four.

Lastly, an attempt was made which almost as far exceeds human credulity to believe as it did human patience to submit to. This was to make us pay as much for existing an hour or two as for existing a whole day; and dressing dinner was introduced as an article, though we left the house before either pot or spit had approached the fire. Here I own my patience failed me, and I became an example of the truth of the observation, "That all tyranny and oppression may be carried too far, and that a yoke may be made too intolerable for the neck of the tamest slave." When I remonstrated, with some warmth, against this grievance, Mrs. Francis gave me a look, and left the room without making any answer. She returned in a minute, running to me with pen, ink, and paper, in her hand, and desired me to make my own bill; "for she hoped," she said "I did not expect that her house was to be dirtied, and her goods spoiled and consumed for nothing. The whole is but thirteen shillings. Can gentlefolks lie a whole night at a public-house for less? If they can I am sure it is time to give off being a landlady: but pay me what you please; I would have people know that I value money as little as other folks. But I was always a fool, as I says to my husband, and never knows which side my bread is buttered of. And yet, to be sure, your honor shall be my warning not to be bit so again. Some folks knows better than other some how to make their bills. Candles! why yes, to be sure; why should not travelers pay for candles? I am sure I pays for my candles, and the chandler pays the king's majesty for them; and if he did not I must, so as it comes to the same thing in the end. To be sure I am out of sixteens at present, but these burn as white and as clear, though not quite so large. I expects my chandler here soon, or I would send to Portsmouth, if your honor was to stay any time longer. But when folks stays only for a wind, you knows there can be no dependence on such!" Here she put on a little slyness of aspect, and seemed willing to submit to interruption. I interrupted her accordingly by throwing down half a guinea, and declared I had no more English money, which was indeed true; and, as she could not immediately change the thirty-six shilling pieces, it put a final end to the dispute. Mrs. Francis soon left the room, and we soon after left the house; nor would this good woman see us or wish us a good voyage. I must not, however, quit this place, where we had been so ill-treated, without doing it impartial justice, and recording what may, with the strictest truth, be said in its favor.

First, then, as to its situation, it is, I think, most delightful, and in the most pleasant spot in the whole island. It is true it wants the advantage of that beautiful river which leads from Newport to Cowes; but the prospect here extending to the sea, and taking in Portsmouth, Spithead, and St. Helen's, would be more than a recompense for the loss of the Thames itself, even in the most delightful part of Berkshire or Buckinghamshire, though another Denham, or another Pope, should unite in celebrating it. For my own part, I confess myself so entirely fond of a sea prospect, that I think nothing on the land can equal it; and if it be set off with shipping, I desire to borrow no ornament from the terra firma. A fleet of ships is, in my opinion, the noblest object which the art of man hath ever produced; and far beyond the power of those architects who deal in brick, in stone, or in marble.

When the late Sir Robert Walpole, one of the best of men and of ministers, used to equip us a yearly fleet at Spithead, his enemies of taste must have allowed that he, at least, treated the nation with a fine sight for their money. A much finer, indeed, than the same expense in an encampment could have produced. For what indeed is the best idea which the prospect of a number of huts can furnish to the mind, but of a number of men forming themselves into a society before the art of building more substantial houses was known? This, perhaps, would be agreeable enough; but, in truth, there is a much worse idea ready to step in before it, and that is of a body of cut-throats, the supports of tyranny, the invaders of the just liberties and properties of mankind, the plunderers of the industrious, the ravishers of the chaste, the murderers of the innocent, and, in a word, the destroyers of the plenty, the peace, and the safety, of their fellow-creatures.

And what, it may be said, are these men-of-war which seem so delightful an object to our eyes? Are they not alike the support of tyranny and oppression of innocence, carrying with them desolation and ruin wherever their masters please to send them? This is indeed too true; and however the ship of war may, in its bulk and equipment, exceed the honest merchantman, I heartily wish there was no necessity for it; for, though I must own the superior beauty of the object on one side, I am more pleased with the superior excellence of the idea which I can raise in my mind on the other, while I reflect on the art and industry of mankind engaged in the daily improvements of commerce to the mutual benefit of all countries, and to the establishment and happiness of social life. This pleasant village is situated on a gentle ascent from the water, whence it affords that charming prospect I have above described. Its soil is a gravel, which, assisted with its declivity, preserves it always so dry that immediately after the most violent rain a fine lady may walk without wetting her silken shoes. The fertility of the place is apparent from its extraordinary verdure, and it is so shaded with large and flourishing elms, that its narrow lanes are a natural grove or walk, which, in the regularity of its plantation, vies with the power of art, and in its wanton exuberancy greatly exceeds it.

In a field in the ascent of this hill, about a quarter of a mile from the sea, stands a neat little chapel. It is very small, but adequate to the number of inhabitants; for the parish doth not seem to contain above thirty houses.

At about two miles distant from this parish lives that polite and good lady to whose kindness we were so much obliged. It is placed on a hill whose bottom is washed by the sea, and which from its eminence at top, commands a view of great part of the island as well as it does that of the opposite shore. This house was formerly built by one Boyce, who, from a blacksmith at Gosport, became possessed, by great success in smuggling, of forty thousand pound. With part of this he purchased an estate here, and, by chance probably, fixed on this spot for building a large house. Perhaps the convenience of carrying on his business, to which it is so well adapted, might dictate the situation to him. We can hardly, at least, attribute it to the same taste with which he furnished his house, or at least his library, by sending an order to a bookseller in London to pack him up five hundred pounds' worth of his handsomest books. They tell here several almost incredible stories of the ignorance, the folly, and the pride, which this poor man and his wife discovered during the short continuance of his prosperity; for he did not long escape the sharp eyes of the revenue solicitors, and was, by extents from the court of Exchequer, soon reduced below his original state to that of confinement in the Fleet. All his effects were sold, and among the rest his books, by an auction at Portsmouth, for a very small price; for the bookseller was now discovered to have been perfectly a master of his trade, and, relying on Mr. Boyce's finding little time to read, had sent him not only the most lasting wares of his shop, but duplicates of the same, under different titles.

His estate and house were purchased by a gentleman of these parts, whose widow now enjoys them, and who hath improved them, particularly her gardens, with so elegant a taste, that the painter who would assist his imagination in the composition of a most exquisite landscape, or the poet who would describe an earthly paradise, could nowhere furnish themselves with a richer pattern.

We left this place about eleven in the morning, and were again conveyed, with more sunshine than wind, aboard our ship.

Whence our captain had acquired his power of prophecy, when he promised us and himself a prosperous wind, I will not determine; it is sufficient to observe that he was a false prophet, and that the weathercocks continued to point as before. He would not, however, so easily give up his skill in prediction. He persevered in asserting that the wind was changed, and, having weighed his anchor, fell down that afternoon to St. Helen's, which was at about the distance of five miles; and whither his friend the tide, in defiance of the wind, which was most manifestly against him, softly wafted him in as many hours.

Here, about seven in the evening, before which time we could not procure it, we sat down to regale ourselves with some roasted venison, which was much better dressed than we imagined it would be, and an excellent cold pasty which my wife had made at Ryde, and which we had reserved uncut to eat on board our ship, whither we all cheerfully exulted in being returned from the presence of Mrs. Francis, who, by the exact resemblance she bore to a fury, seemed to have been with no great propriety settled in paradise.

Friday, July 24.—As we passed by Spithead on the preceding evening we saw the two regiments of soldiers who were just returned from Gibraltar and Minorca; and this day a lieutenant belonging to one of them, who was the captain's nephew, came to pay a visit to his uncle. He was what is called by some a very pretty fellow; indeed, much too pretty a fellow at his years; for he was turned of thirty-four, though his address and conversation would have become him more before he had reached twenty. In his conversation, it is true, there was something military enough, as it consisted chiefly of oaths, and of the great actions and wise sayings of Jack, and Will, and Tom of our regiment, a phrase eternally in his mouth; and he seemed to conclude that it conveyed to all the officers such a degree of public notoriety and importance that it entitled him like the head of a profession, or a first minister, to be the subject of conversation among those who had not the least personal acquaintance with him. This did not much surprise me, as I have seen several examples of the same; but the defects in his address, especially to the women, were so great that they seemed absolutely inconsistent with the behavior of a pretty fellow, much less of one in a red coat; and yet, besides having been eleven years in the army, he had had, as his uncle informed me, an education in France. This, I own, would have appeared to have been absolutely thrown away had not his animal spirits, which were likewise thrown away upon him in great abundance, borne the visible stamp of the growth of that country. The character to which he had an indisputable title was that of a merry fellow; so very merry was he that he laughed at everything he said, and always before he spoke. Possibly, indeed, he often laughed at what he did not utter, for every speech begun with a laugh, though it did not always end with a jest. There was no great analogy between the characters of the uncle and the nephew, and yet they seemed entirely to agree in enjoying the honor which the red-coat did to his family. This the uncle expressed with great pleasure in his countenance, and seemed desirous of showing all present the honor which he had for his nephew, who, on his side, was at some pains to convince us of his concurring in this opinion, and at the same time of displaying the contempt he had for the parts, as well as the occupation of his uncle, which he seemed to think reflected some disgrace on himself, who was a member of that profession which makes every man a gentleman. Not that I would be understood to insinuate that the nephew endeavored to shake off or disown his uncle, or indeed to keep him at any distance. On the contrary, he treated him with the utmost familiarity, often calling him Dick, and dear Dick, and old Dick, and frequently beginning an oration with D—n me, Dick.

All this condescension on the part of the young man was received with suitable marks of complaisance and obligation by the old one; especially when it was attended with evidences of the same familiarity with general officers and other persons of rank; one of whom, in particular, I know to have the pride and insolence of the devil himself, and who, without some strong bias of interest, is no more liable to converse familiarly with a lieutenant than of being mistaken in his judgment of a fool; which was not, perhaps, so certainly the case of the worthy lieutenant, who, in declaring to us the qualifications which recommended men to his countenance and conversation, as well as what effectually set a bar to all hopes of that honor, exclaimed, "No, sir, by the d— I hate all fools— No, d—n me, excuse me for that. That's a little too much, old Dick. There are two or three officers of our regiment whom I know to be fools; but d—n me if I am ever seen in their company. If a man hath a fool of a relation, Dick, you know he can't help that, old boy." Such jokes as these the old man not only tools in good part, but glibly gulped down the whole narrative of his nephew; nor did he, I am convinced, in the least doubt of our as readily swallowing the same. This made him so charmed with the lieutenant, that it is probable we should have been pestered with him the whole evening, had not the north wind, dearer to our sea-captain even than this glory of his family, sprung suddenly up, and called aloud to him to weigh his anchor. While this ceremony was performing, the sea-captain ordered out his boat to row the land-captain to shore; not indeed on an uninhabited island, but one which, in this part, looked but little better, not presenting us the view of a single house. Indeed, our old friend, when his boat returned on shore, perhaps being no longer able to stifle his envy of the superiority of his nephew, told us with a smile that the young man had a good five mile to walk before he could be accommodated with a passage to Portsmouth.

It appeared now that the captain had been only mistaken in the date of his prediction, by placing the event a day earlier than it happened; for the wind which now arose was not only favorable but brisk, and was no sooner in reach of our sails than it swept us away by the back of the Isle of Wight, and, having in the night carried us by Christchurch and Peveral-point, brought us the next noon, Saturday, July 25, oft the island of Portland, so famous for the smallness and sweetness of its mutton, of which a leg seldom weighs four pounds. We would have bought a sheep, but our captain would not permit it; though he needed not have been in such a hurry, for presently the wind, I will not positively assert in resentment of his surliness, showed him a dog's trick, and slyly slipped back again to his summer-house in the south-west.

The captain now grew outrageous, and, declaring open war with the wind, took a resolution, rather more bold than wise, of sailing in defiance of it, and in its teeth. He swore he would let go his anchor no more, but would beat the sea while he had either yard or sail left. He accordingly stood from the shore, and made so large a tack that before night, though he seemed to advance but little on his way, he was got out of sight of land.

Towards evening the wind began, in the captain's own language, and indeed it freshened so much, that before ten it blew a perfect hurricane. The captain having got, as he supposed, to a safe distance, tacked again towards the English shore; and now the wind veered a point only in his favor, and continued to blow with such violence, that the ship ran above eight knots or miles an hour during this whole day and tempestuous night till bed-time. I was obliged to betake myself once more to my solitude, for my women were again all down in their sea-sickness, and the captain was busy on deck; for he began to grow uneasy, chiefly, I believe, because he did not well know where he was, and would, I am convinced, have been very glad to have been in Portland-road, eating some sheep's-head broth.

Having contracted no great degree of good-humor by living a whole day alone, without a single soul to converse with, I took but ill physic to purge it off, by a bed-conversation with the captain, who, amongst many bitter lamentations of his fate, and protesting he had more patience than a Job, frequently intermixed summons to the commanding officer on the deck, who now happened to be one Morrison, a carpenter, the only fellow that had either common sense or common civility in the ship. Of Morrison he inquired every quarter of an hour concerning the state of affairs: the wind, the care of the ship, and other matters of navigation. The frequency of these summons, as well as the solicitude with which they were made, sufficiently testified the state of the captain's mind; he endeavored to conceal it, and would have given no small alarm to a man who had either not learned what it is to die, or known what it is to be miserable. And my dear wife and child must pardon me, if what I did not conceive to be any great evil to myself I was not much terrified with the thoughts of happening to them; in truth, I have often thought they are both too good and too gentle to be trusted to the power of any man I know, to whom they could possibly be so trusted.

Can I say then I had no fear? indeed I cannot. Reader, I was afraid for thee, lest thou shouldst have been deprived of that pleasure thou art now enjoying; and that I should not live to draw out on paper that military character which thou didst peruse in the journal of yesterday.

From all these fears we were relieved, at six in the morning, by the arrival of Mr. Morrison, who acquainted us that he was sure he beheld land very near; for he could not see half a mile, by reason of the haziness of the weather. This land he said was, he believed, the Berry-head, which forms one side of Torbay: the captain declared that it was impossible, and swore, on condition he was right, he would give him his mother for a maid. A forfeit which became afterwards strictly due and payable; for the captain, whipping on his night-gown, ran up without his breeches, and within half an hour returning into the cabin, wished me joy of our lying safe at anchor in the bay.

Sunday, July 26.—Things now began to put on an aspect very different from what they had lately worn; the news that the ship had almost lost its mizzen, and that we had procured very fine clouted cream and fresh bread and butter from the shore, restored health and spirits to our women, and we all sat down to a very cheerful breakfast. But, however pleasant our stay promised to be here, we were all desirous it should be short: I resolved immediately to despatch my man into the country to purchase a present of cider, for my friends of that which is called Southam, as well as to take with me a hogshead of it to Lisbon; for it is, in my opinion, much more delicious than that which is the growth of Herefordshire. I purchased three hogsheads for five pounds ten shillings, all which I should have scarce thought worth mentioning, had I not believed it might be of equal service to the honest farmer who sold it me, and who is by the neighboring gentlemen reputed to deal in the very best; and to the reader, who, from ignorance of the means of providing better for himself, swallows at a dearer rate the juice of Middlesex turnip, instead of that Vinum Pomonae which Mr. Giles Leverance of Cheeshurst, near Dartmouth in Devon, will, at the price of forty shillings per hogshead, send in double casks to any part of the world. Had the wind been very sudden in shifting, I had lost my cider by an attempt of a boatman to exact, according to custom. He required five shillings for conveying my man a mile and a half to the shore, and four more if he stayed to bring him back. This I thought to be such insufferable impudence that I ordered him to be immediately chased from the ship, without any answer. Indeed, there are few inconveniences that I would not rather encounter than encourage the insolent demands of these wretches, at the expense of my own indignation, of which I own they are not the only objects, but rather those who purchase a paltry convenience by encouraging them. But of this I have already spoken very largely. I shall conclude, therefore, with the leave which this fellow took of our ship; saying he should know it again, and would not put off from the shore to relieve it in any distress whatever. It will, doubtless, surprise many of my readers to hear that, when we lay at anchor within a mile or two of a town several days together, and even in the most temperate weather, we should frequently want fresh provisions and herbage, and other emoluments of the shore, as much as if we had been a hundred leagues from land. And this too while numbers of boats were in our sight, whose owners get their livelihood by rowing people up and down, and could be at any time summoned by a signal to our assistance, and while the captain had a little boat of his own, with men always ready to row it at his command.

This, however, hath been partly accounted for already by the imposing disposition of the people, who asked so much more than the proper price of their labor. And as to the usefulness of the captain's boat, it requires to be a little expatiated upon, as it will tend to lay open some of the grievances which demand the utmost regard of our legislature, as they affect the most valuable part of the king's subjects—those by whom the commerce of the nation is carried into execution. Our captain then, who was a very good and experienced seaman, having been above thirty years the master of a vessel, part of which he had served, so he phrased it, as commander of a privateer, and had discharged himself with great courage and conduct, and with as great success, discovered the utmost aversion to the sending his boat ashore whenever we lay wind-bound in any of our harbors. This aversion did not arise from any fear of wearing out his boat by using it, but was, in truth, the result of experience, that it was easier to send his men on shore than to recall them. They acknowledged him to be their master while they remained on shipboard, but did not allow his power to extend to the shores, where they had no sooner set their foot than every man became sui juris, and thought himself at full liberty to return when he pleased. Now it is not any delight that these fellows have in the fresh air or verdant fields on the land. Every one of them would prefer his ship and his hammock to all the sweets of Arabia the Happy; but, unluckily for them, there are in every seaport in England certain houses whose chief livelihood depends on providing entertainment for the gentlemen of the jacket. For this purpose they are always well furnished with those cordial liquors which do immediately inspire the heart with gladness, banishing all careful thoughts, and indeed all others, from the mind, and opening the mouth with songs of cheerfulness and thanksgiving for the many wonderful blessings with which a seafaring life overflows.

For my own part, however whimsical it may appear, I confess I have thought the strange story of Circe in the Odyssey no other than an ingenious allegory, in which Homer intended to convey to his countrymen the same kind of instruction which we intend to communicate to our own in this digression. As teaching the art of war to the Greeks was the plain design of the Iliad, so was teaching them the art of navigation the no less manifest intention of the Odyssey. For the improvement of this, their situation was most excellently adapted; and accordingly we find Thucydides, in the beginning of his history, considers the Greeks as a set of pirates or privateers, plundering each other by sea. This being probably the first institution of commerce before the Ars Cauponaria was invented, and merchants, instead of robbing, began to cheat and outwit each other, and by degrees changed the Metabletic, the only kind of traffic allowed by Aristotle in his Politics, into the Chrematistic.

By this allegory then I suppose Ulysses to have been the captain of a merchant-ship, and Circe some good ale-wife, who made his crew drunk with the spirituous liquors of those days. With this the transformation into swine, as well as all other incidents of the fable, will notably agree; and thus a key will be found out for unlocking the whole mystery, and forging at least some meaning to a story which, at present, appears very strange and absurd.

Hence, moreover, will appear the very near resemblance between the sea-faring men of all ages and nations; and here perhaps may be established the truth and justice of that observation, which will occur oftener than once in this voyage, that all human flesh is not the same flesh, but that there is one kind of flesh of landmen, and another of seamen.

Philosophers, divines, and others, who have treated the gratification of human appetites with contempt, have, among other instances, insisted very strongly on that satiety which is so apt to overtake them even in the very act of enjoyment. And here they more particularly deserve our attention, as most of them may be supposed to speak from their own experience, and very probably gave us their lessons with a full stomach. Thus hunger and thirst, whatever delight they may afford while we are eating and drinking, pass both away from us with the plate and the cup; and though we should imitate the Romans, if, indeed, they were such dull beasts, which I can scarce believe, to unload the belly like a dung-pot, in order to fill it again with another load, yet would the pleasure be so considerably lessened that it would scarce repay us the trouble of purchasing it with swallowing a basin of camomile tea. A second haunch of venison, or a second dose of turtle, would hardly allure a city glutton with its smell. Even the celebrated Jew himself, when well filled with calipash and calipee, goes contentedly home to tell his money, and expects no more pleasure from his throat during the next twenty-four hours. Hence I suppose Dr. South took that elegant comparison of the joys of a speculative man to the solemn silence of an Archimedes over a problem, and those of a glutton to the stillness of a sow at her wash. A simile which, if it became the pulpit at all, could only become it in the afternoon. Whereas in those potations which the mind seems to enjoy, rather than the bodily appetite, there is happily no such satiety; but the more a man drinks, the more he desires; as if, like Mark Anthony in Dryden, his appetite increased with feeding, and this to such an immoderate degree, ut nullus sit desiderio aut pudor aut modus. Hence, as with the gang of Captain Ulysses, ensues so total a transformation, that the man no more continues what he was. Perhaps he ceases for a time to be at all; or, though he may retain the same outward form and figure he had before, yet is his nobler part, as we are taught to call it, so changed, that, instead of being the same man, he scarce remembers what he was a few hours before. And this transformation, being once obtained, is so easily preserved by the same potations, which induced no satiety, that the captain in vain sends or goes in quest of his crew. They know him no longer; or, if they do, they acknowledge not his power, having indeed as entirely forgotten themselves as if they had taken a large draught of the river of Lethe.

Nor is the captain always sure of even finding out the place to which Circe hath conveyed them. There are many of those houses in every port-town. Nay, there are some where the sorceress doth not trust only to her drugs; but hath instruments of a different kind to execute her purposes, by whose means the tar is effectually secreted from the knowledge and pursuit of his captain. This would, indeed, be very fatal, was it not for one circumstance; that the sailor is seldom provided with the proper bait for these harpies. However, the contrary sometimes happens, as these harpies will bite at almost anything, and will snap at a pair of silver buttons, or buckles, as surely as at the specie itself. Nay, sometimes they are so voracious, that the very naked hook will go down, and the jolly young sailor is sacrificed for his own sake.

In vain, at such a season as this, would the vows of a pious heathen have prevailed over Neptune, Aeolus, or any other marine deity. In vain would the prayers of a Christian captain be attended with the like success. The wind may change how it pleases while all hands are on shore; the anchor would remain firm in the ground, and the ship would continue in durance, unless, like other forcible prison-breakers, it forcibly got loose for no good purpose. Now, as the favor of winds and courts, and such like, is always to be laid hold on at the very first motion, for within twenty-four hours all may be changed again; so, in the former case, the loss of a day may be the loss of a voyage: for, though it may appear to persons not well skilled in navigation, who see ships meet and sail by each other, that the wind blows sometimes east and west, north and south, backwards and forwards, at the same instant; yet, certain it is that the land is so contrived, that even the same wind will not, like the same horse, always bring a man to the end of his journey; but, that the gale which the mariner prayed heartily for yesterday, he may as heartily deprecate to-morrow; while all use and benefit which would have arisen to him from the westerly wind of to-morrow may be totally lost and thrown away by neglecting the offer of the easterly blast which blows to-day.

Hence ensues grief and disreputation to the innocent captain, loss and disappointment to the worthy merchant, and not seldom great prejudice to the trade of a nation whose manufactures are thus liable to lie unsold in a foreign warehouse the market being forestalled by some rival whose sailors are under a better discipline. To guard against these inconveniences the prudent captain takes every precaution in his power; he makes the strongest contracts with his crew, and thereby binds them so firmly, that none but the greatest or least of men can break through them with impunity; but for one of these two reasons, which I will not determine, the sailor, like his brother fish the eel, is too slippery to be held, and plunges into his element with perfect impunity. To speak a plain truth, there is no trusting to any contract with one whom the wise citizens of London call a bad man; for, with such a one, though your bond be ever so strong, it will prove in the end good for nothing.

What then is to be done in this case? What, indeed, but to call in the assistance of that tremendous magistrate, the justice of peace, who can, and often doth, lay good and bad men in equal durance; and, though he seldom cares to stretch his bonds to what is great, never finds anything too minute for their detention, but will hold the smallest reptile alive so fast in his noose, that he can never get out till he is let drop through it. Why, therefore, upon the breach of those contracts, should not an immediate application be made to the nearest magistrate of this order, who should be empowered to convey the delinquent either to ship or to prison, at the election of the captain, to be fettered by the leg in either place? But, as the case now stands, the condition of this poor captain without any commission, and of this absolute commander without any power, is much worse than we have hitherto shown it to be; for, notwithstanding all the aforesaid contracts to sail in the good ship the Elizabeth, if the sailor should, for better wages, find it more his interest to go on board the better ship the Mary, either before their setting out or on their speedy meeting in some port, he may prefer the latter without any other danger than that of "doing what he ought not to have done," contrary to a rule which he is seldom Christian enough to have much at heart, while the captain is generally too good a Christian to punish a man out of revenge only, when he is to be at a considerable expense for so doing. There are many other deficiencies in our laws relating to maritime affairs, and which would probably have been long since corrected, had we any seamen in the House of Commons. Not that I would insinuate that the legislature wants a supply of many gentlemen in the sea-service; but, as these gentlemen are by their attendance in the house unfortunately prevented from ever going to sea, and there learning what they might communicate to their landed brethren, these latter remain as ignorant in that branch of knowledge as they would be if none but courtiers and fox-hunters had been elected into parliament, without a single fish among them. The following seems to me to be an effect of this kind, and it strikes me the stronger as I remember the case to have happened, and remember it to have been dispunishable. A captain of a trading vessel, of which he was part owner, took in a large freight of oats at Liverpool, consigned to the market at Bearkey: this he carried to a port in Hampshire, and there sold it as his own, and, freighting his vessel with wheat for the port of Cadiz, in Spain, dropped it at Oporto in his way; and there, selling it for his own use, took in a lading of wine, with which he sailed again, and, having converted it in the same manner, together with a large sum of money with which he was intrusted, for the benefit of certain merchants, sold the ship and cargo in another port, and then wisely sat down contented with the fortune he had made, and returned to London to enjoy the remainder of his days, with the fruits of his former labors and a good conscience.

The sum he brought home with him consisted of near six thousand pounds, all in specie, and most of it in that coin which Portugal distributes so liberally over Europe.

He was not yet old enough to be past all sense of pleasure, nor so puffed up with the pride of his good fortune as to overlook his old acquaintances the journeymen tailors, from among whom he had been formerly pressed into the sea-service, and, having there laid the foundation of his future success by his shares in prizes, had afterwards become captain of a trading vessel, in which he purchased an interest, and had soon begun to trade in the honorable manner above mentioned. The captain now took up his residence at an ale-house in Drury-lane, where, having all his money by him in a trunk, he spent about five pounds a day among his old friends the gentlemen and ladies of those parts. The merchant of Liverpool, having luckily had notice from a friend during the blaze of his fortune, did, by the assistance of a justice of peace, without the assistance of the law, recover his whole loss. The captain, however, wisely chose to refund no more; but, perceiving with what hasty strides Envy was pursuing his fortune, he took speedy means to retire out of her reach, and to enjoy the rest of his wealth in an inglorious obscurity; nor could the same justice overtake him time enough to assist a second merchant as he had done the first.

This was a very extraordinary case, and the more so as the ingenious gentleman had steered entirely clear of all crimes in our law. Now, how it comes about that a robbery so very easy to be committed, and to which there is such immediate temptation always before the eyes of these fellows, should receive the encouragement of impunity, is to be accounted for only from the oversight of the legislature, as that oversight can only be, I think, derived from the reasons I have assigned for it.

But I will dwell no longer on this subject. If what I have here said should seem of sufficient consequence to engage the attention of any man in power, and should thus be the means of applying any remedy to the most inveterate evils, at least, I have obtained my whole desire, and shall have lain so long wind-bound in the ports of this kingdom to some purpose. I would, indeed, have this work— which, if I should live to finish it, a matter of no great certainty, if indeed of any great hope to me, will be probably the last I shall ever undertake—to produce some better end than the mere diversion of the reader.

Monday.—This day our captain went ashore, to dine with a gentleman who lives in these parts, and who so exactly resembles the character given by Homer of Axylus, that the only difference I can trace between them is, the one, living by the highway, erected his hospitality chiefly in favor of land-travelers; and the other, living by the water-side, gratified his humanity by accommodating the wants of the mariner.

In the evening our commander received a visit from a brother bashaw, who lay wind-bound in the same harbor. This latter captain was a Swiss. He was then master of a vessel bound to Guinea, and had formerly been a privateering, when our own hero was employed in the same laudable service. The honesty and freedom of the Switzer, his vivacity, in which he was in no respect inferior to his near neighbors the French, the awkward and affected politeness, which was likewise of French extraction, mixed with the brutal roughness of the English tar—for he had served under the colors of this nation and his crew had been of the same—made such an odd variety, such a hotch-potch of character, that I should have been much diverted with him, had not his voice, which was as loud as a speaking-trumpet, unfortunately made my head ache. The noise which he conveyed into the deaf ears of his brother captain, who sat on one side of him, the soft addresses with which, mixed with awkward bows, he saluted the ladies on the other, were so agreeably contrasted, that a man must not only have been void of all taste of humor, and insensible of mirth, but duller than Cibber is represented in the Dunciad, who could be unentertained with him a little while; for, I confess, such entertainments should always be very short, as they are very liable to pall. But he suffered not this to happen at present; for, having given us his company a quarter of an hour only, he retired, after many apologies for the shortness of his visit.

Tuesday.—The wind being less boisterous than it had hitherto been since our arrival here, several fishing-boats, which the tempestuous weather yesterday had prevented from working, came on board us with fish. This was so fresh, so good in kind, and so very cheap, that we supplied ourselves in great numbers, among which were very large soles at fourpence a pair, and whitings of almost a preposterous size at ninepence a score. The only fish which bore any price was a john doree, as it is called. I bought one of at least four pounds weight for as many shillings. It resembles a turbot in shape, but exceeds it in firmness and flavor. The price had the appearance of being considerable when opposed to the extraordinary cheapness of others of value, but was, in truth, so very reasonable when estimated by its goodness, that it left me under no other surprise than how the gentlemen of this country, not greatly eminent for the delicacy of their taste, had discovered the preference of the doree to all other fish: but I was informed that Mr. Quin, whose distinguishing tooth hath been so justly celebrated, had lately visited Plymouth, and had done those honors to the doree which are so justly due to it from that sect of modern philosophers who, with Sir Epicure Mammon, or Sir Epicure Quin, their head, seem more to delight in a fish-pond than in a garden, as the old Epicureans are said to have done.

Unfortunately for the fishmongers of London, the doree resides only in those seas; for, could any of this company but convey one to the temple of luxury under the Piazza, where Macklin the high-priest daily serves up his rich offerings to that goddess, great would be the reward of that fishmonger, in blessings poured down upon him from the goddess, as great would his merit be towards the high-priest, who could never be thought to overrate such valuable incense.

And here, having mentioned the extreme cheapness of fish in the Devonshire sea, and given some little hint of the extreme dearness with which this commodity is dispensed by those who deal in it in London, I cannot pass on without throwing forth an observation or two, with the same view with which I have scattered my several remarks through this voyage, sufficiently satisfied in having finished my life, as I have probably lost it, in the service of my country, from the best of motives, though it should be attended with the worst of success. Means are always in our power; ends are very seldom so.

Of all the animal foods with which man is furnished, there are none so plenty as fish. A little rivulet, that glides almost unperceived through a vast tract of rich land, will support more hundreds with the flesh of its inhabitants than the meadow will nourish individuals. But if this be true of rivers, it is much truer of the sea-shores, which abound with such immense variety of fish that the curious fisherman, after he hath made his draught, often culls only the daintiest part and leaves the rest of his prey to perish on the shore. If this be true it would appear, I think, that there is nothing which might be had in such abundance, and consequently so cheap, as fish, of which Nature seems to have provided such inexhaustible stores with some peculiar design. In the production of terrestrial animals she proceeds with such slowness, that in the larger kind a single female seldom produces more than one a-year, and this again requires three, for, or five years more to bring it to perfection. And though the lesser quadrupeds, those of the wild kind particularly, with the birds, do multiply much faster, yet can none of these bear any proportion with the aquatic animals, of whom every female matrix is furnished with an annual offspring almost exceeding the power of numbers, and which, in many instances at least, a single year is capable of bringing to some degree of maturity.

What then ought in general to be so plentiful, what so cheap, as fish? What then so properly the food of the poor? So in many places they are, and so might they always be in great cities, which are always situated near the sea, or on the conflux of large rivers. How comes it then, to look no farther abroad for instances, that in our city of London the case is so far otherwise that, except that of sprats, there is not one poor palate in a hundred that knows the taste of fish?

It is true indeed that this taste is generally of such excellent flavor that it exceeds the power of French cookery to treat the palates of the rich with anything more exquisitely delicate; so that was fish the common food of the poor it might put them too much upon an equality with their betters in the great article of eating, in which, at present, in the opinion of some, the great difference in happiness between man and man consists. But this argument I shall treat with the utmost disdain: for if ortolans were as big as buzzards, and at the same time as plenty as sparrows, I should hold it yet reasonable to indulge the poor with the dainty, and that for this cause especially, that the rich would soon find a sparrow, if as scarce as an ortolan, to be much the greater, as it would certainly be the rarer, dainty of the two.

Vanity or scarcity will be always the favorite of luxury; but honest hunger will be satisfied with plenty. Not to search deeper into the cause of the evil, I should think it abundantly sufficient to propose the remedies of it. And, first, I humbly submit the absolute necessity of immediately hanging all the fishmongers within the bills of mortality; and, however it might have been some time ago the opinion of mild and temporizing men that the evil complained of might be removed by gentler methods, I suppose at this day there are none who do not see the impossibility of using such with any effect. Cuncta prius tentanda might have been formerly urged with some plausibility, but cuncta prius tentata may now be replied: for surely, if a few monopolizing fishmongers could defeat that excellent scheme of the Westminster market, to the erecting which so many justices of peace, as well as other wise and learned men, did so vehemently apply themselves, that they might be truly said not only to have laid the whole strength of their heads, but of their shoulders too, to the business, it would be a vain endeavor for any other body of men to attempt to remove so stubborn a nuisance.

If it should be doubted whether we can bring this case within the letter of any capital law now subsisting, I am ashamed to own it cannot; for surely no crime better deserves such punishment; but the remedy may, nevertheless, be immediate; and if a law was made at the beginning of next session, to take place immediately, by which the starving thousands of poor was declared to be felony, without benefit of clergy, the fishmongers would be hanged before the end of the session. A second method of filling the mouths of the poor, if not with loaves at least with fishes, is to desire the magistrates to carry into execution one at least out of near a hundred acts of parliament, for preserving the small fry of the river of Thames, by which means as few fish would satisfy thousands as may now be devoured by a small number of individnals. But while a fisherman can break through the strongest meshes of an act of parliament, we may be assured he will learn so to contrive his own meshes that the smallest fry will not be able to swim through them.

Other methods may, we doubt not, be suggested by those who shall attentively consider the evil here hinted at; but we have dwelt too long on it already, and shall conclude with observing that it is difficult to affirm whether the atrocity of the evil itself, the facility of curing it, or the shameful neglect of the cure, be the more scandalous or more astonishing.

After having, however, gloriously regaled myself with this food, I was washing it down with some good claret with my wife and her friend, in the cabin, when the captain's valet-de-chambre, head cook, house and ship steward, footman in livery and out on't, secretary and fore-mast man, all burst into the cabin at once, being, indeed, all but one person, and, without saying, by your leave, began to pack half a hogshead of small beer in bottles, the necessary consequence of which must have been either a total stop to conversation at that cheerful season when it is most agreeable, or the admitting that polyonymous officer aforesaid to the participation of it. I desired him therefore to delay his purpose a little longer, but he refused to grant my request; nor was he prevailed on to quit the room till he was threatened with having one bottle to pack more than his number, which then happened to stand empty within my reach. With these menaces he retired at last, but not without muttering some menaces on his side, and which, to our great terror, he failed not to put into immediate execution.

Our captain was gone to dinner this day with his Swiss brother; and, though he was a very sober man, was a little elevated with some champagne, which, as it cost the Swiss little or nothing, he dispensed at his table more liberally than our hospitable English noblemen put about those bottles, which the ingenious Peter Taylor teaches a led captain to avoid by distinguishing by the name of that generous liquor, which all humble companions are taught to postpone to the flavor of methuen, or honest port.

While our two captains were thus regaling themselves, and celebrating their own heroic exploits with all the inspiration which the liquor, at least, of wit could afford them, the polyonymous officer arrived, and, being saluted by the name of Honest Tom, was ordered to sit down and take his glass before he delivered his message; for every sailor is by turns his captain's mate over a cann, except only that captain bashaw who presides in a man-of-war, and who upon earth has no other mate, unless it be another of the same bashaws. Tom had no sooner swallowed his draught than he hastily began his narrative, and faithfully related what had happened on board our ship; we say faithfully, though from what happened it may be suspected that Tom chose to add perhaps only five or six immaterial circumstances, as is always I believe the case, and may possibly have been done by me in relating this very story, though it happened not many hours ago.

No sooner was the captain informed of the interruption which had been given to his officer, and indeed to his orders, for he thought no time so convenient as that of his absence for causing any confusion in the cabin, than he leaped with such haste from his chair that he had like to have broke his sword, with which he always begirt himself when he walked out of his ship, and sometimes when he walked about in it; at the same time, grasping eagerly that other implement called a cockade, which modern soldiers wear on their helmets with the same view as the ancients did their crests—to terrify the enemy he muttered something, but so inarticulately that the word DAMN was only intelligible; he then hastily took leave of the Swiss captain, who was too well bred to press his stay on such an occasion, and leaped first from the ship to his boat, and then from his boat to his own ship, with as much fierceness in his looks as he had ever expressed on boarding his defenseless prey in the honorable calling of a privateer. Having regained the middle deck, he paused a moment while Tom and others loaded themselves with bottles, and then descending into the cabin exclaimed with a thundering voice, "D—n me, why arn't the bottles stowed in, according to my orders?"

I answered him very mildly that I had prevented his man from doing it, as it was at an inconvenient time to me, and as in his absence, at least, I esteemed the cabin to be my own. "Your cabin!" repeated he many times; "no, d—n me! 'tis my cabin. Your cabin! d—n me! I have brought my hogs to a fair market. I suppose indeed you think it your cabin, and your ship, by your commanding in it; but I will command in it, d—n me! I will show the world I am the commander, and nobody but I! Did you think I sold you the command of my ship for that pitiful thirty pounds? I wish I had not seen you nor your thirty pounds aboard of her." He then repeated the words thirty pounds often, with great disdain, and with a contempt which I own the sum did not seem to deserve in my eye, either in itself or on the present occasion; being, indeed, paid for the freight of — — weight of human flesh, which is above fifty per cent dearer than the freight of any other luggage, whilst in reality it takes up less room; in fact, no room at all.

In truth, the sum was paid for nothing more than for a liberty to six persons (two of them servants) to stay on board a ship while she sails from one port to another, every shilling of which comes clear into the captain's pocket. Ignorant people may perhaps imagine, especially when they are told that the captain is obliged to sustain them, that their diet at least is worth something, which may probably be now and then so far the case as to deduct a tenth part from the net profits on this account; but it was otherwise at present; for when I had contracted with the captain at a price which I by no means thought moderate, I had some content in thinking I should have no more to pay for my voyage; but I was whispered that it was expected the passengers should find themselves in several things; such as tea, wine, and such like; and particularly that gentlemen should stow of the latter a much larger quantity than they could use, in order to leave the remainder as a present to the captain at the end of the voyage; and it was expected likewise that gentlemen should put aboard some fresh stores, and the more of such things were put aboard the welcomer they would be to the captain.

I was prevailed with by these hints to follow the advice proposed; and accordingly, besides tea and a large hamper of wine, with several hams and tongues, I caused a number of live chickens and sheep to be conveyed aboard; in truth, treble the quantity of provisions which would have supported the persons I took with me, had the voyage continued three weeks, as it was supposed, with a bare possibility, it might.

Indeed it continued much longer; but as this was occasioned by our being wind-bound in our own ports, it was by no means of any ill consequence to the captain, as the additional stores of fish, fresh meat, butter, bread, etc., which I constantly laid in, greatly exceeded the consumption, and went some way in maintaining the ship's crew. It is true I was not obliged to do this; but it seemed to be expected; for the captain did not think himself obliged to do it, and I can truly say I soon ceased to expect it of him. He had, I confess, on board a number of fowls and ducks sufficient for a West India voyage; all of them, as he often said, "Very fine birds, and of the largest breed." This I believe was really the fact, and I can add that they were all arrived at the full perfection of their size. Nor was there, I am convinced, any want of provisions of a more substantial kind; such as dried beef, pork, and fish; so that the captain seemed ready to perform his contract, and amply to provide for his passengers. What I did then was not from necessity, but, perhaps, from a less excusable motive, and was by no means chargeable to the account of the captain.

But, let the motive have been what it would, the consequence was still the same; and this was such that I am firmly persuaded the whole pitiful thirty pounds came pure and neat into the captain's pocket, and not only so, but attended with the value of ten pound more in sundries into the bargain. I must confess myself therefore at a loss how the epithet PITIFUL came to be annexed to the above sum; for, not being a pitiful price for what it was given, I cannot conceive it to be pitiful in itself; nor do I believe it is thought by the greatest men in the kingdom; none of whom would scruple to search for it in the dirtiest kennel, where they had only a reasonable hope of success. How, therefore, such a sum should acquire the idea of pitiful in the eyes of the master of a ship seems not easy to be accounted for; since it appears more likely to produce in him ideas of a different kind. Some men, perhaps, are no more sincere in the contempt for it which they express than others in their contempt of money in general; and I am the rather inclined to this persuasion, as I have seldom heard of either who have refused or refunded this their despised object. Besides, it is sometimes impossible to believe these professions, as every action of the man's life is a contradiction to it. Who can believe a tradesman who says he would not tell his name for the profit he gets by the selling such a parcel of goods, when he hath told a thousand lies in order to get it? Pitiful, indeed, is often applied to an object not absolutely, but comparatively with our expectations, or with a greater object: in which sense it is not easy to set any bounds to the use of the word. Thus, a handful of halfpence daily appear pitiful to a porter, and a handful of silver to a drawer. The latter, I am convinced, at a polite tavern, will not tell his name (for he will not give you any answer) under the price of gold. And in this sense thirty pound may be accounted pitiful by the lowest mechanic.

One difficulty only seems to occur, and that is this: how comes it that, if the profits of the meanest arts are so considerable, the professors of them are not richer than we generally see them? One answer to this shall suffice. Men do not become rich by what they get, but by what they keep. He who is worth no more than his annual wages or salary, spends the whole; he will be always a beggar let his income be what it will, and so will be his family when he dies. This we see daily to be the case of ecclesiastics, who, during their lives, are extremely well provided for, only because they desire to maintain the honor of the cloth by living like gentlemen, which would, perhaps, be better maintained by living unlike them.

But, to return from so long a digression, to which the use of so improper an epithet gave occasion, and to which the novelty of the subject allured, I will make the reader amends by concisely telling him that the captain poured forth such a torrent of abuse that I very hastily and very foolishly resolved to quit the ship.

I gave immediate orders to summon a hoy to carry me that evening to Dartmouth, without considering any consequence. Those orders I gave in no very low voice, so that those above stairs might possibly conceive there was more than one master in the cabin. In the same tone I likewise threatened the captain with that which, he afterwards said, he feared more than any rock or quicksand. Nor can we wonder at this when we are told he had been twice obliged to bring to and cast anchor there before, and had neither time escaped without the loss of almost his whole cargo.

The most distant sound of law thus frightened a man who had often, I am convinced, heard numbers of cannon roar round him with intrepidity. Nor did he sooner see the hoy approaching the vessel than he ran down again into the cabin, and, his rage being perfectly subsided, he tumbled on his knees, and a little too abjectly implored for mercy.

I did not suffer a brave man and an old man to remain a moment in this posture, but I immediately forgave him.

And here, that I may not be thought the sly trumpeter of my own praises, I do utterly disclaim all praise on the occasion. Neither did the greatness of my mind dictate, nor the force of my Christianity exact, this forgiveness. To speak truth, I forgave him from a motive which would make men much more forgiving if they were much wiser than they are, because it was convenient for me so to do.

Wednesday.—This morning the captain dressed himself in scarlet in order to pay a visit to a Devonshire squire, to whom a captain of a ship is a guest of no ordinary consequence, as he is a stranger and a gentleman, who hath seen a great deal of the world in foreign parts, and knows all the news of the times.

The squire, therefore, was to send his boat for the captain, but a most unfortunate accident happened; for, as the wind was extremely rough and against the hoy, while this was endeavoring to avail itself of great seamanship in hauling up against the wind, a sudden squall carried off sail and yard, or at least so disabled them that they were no longer of any use and unable to reach the ship; but the captain, from the deck, saw his hopes of venison disappointed, and was forced either to stay on board his ship, or to hoist forth his own long-boat, which he could not prevail with himself to think of, though the smell of the venison had had twenty times its attraction. He did, indeed, love his ship as his wife, and his boats as children, and never willingly trusted the latter, poor things! to the dangers of the sea.

To say truth, notwithstanding the strict rigor with which he preserved the dignity of his stations and the hasty impatience with which he resented any affront to his person or orders, disobedience to which he could in no instance brook in any person on board. he was one of the best natured fellows alive. He acted the part of a father to his sailors; he expressed great tenderness for any of them when ill, and never suffered any the least work of supererogation to go unrewarded by a glass of gin. He even extended his humanity, if I may so call it, to animals, and even his cats and kittens had large shares in his affections.

An instance of which we saw this evening, when the cat, which had shown it could not be drowned, was found suffocated under a feather-bed in the cabin. I will not endeavor to describe his lamentations with more prolixity than barely by saying they were grievous, and seemed to have some mixture of the Irish howl in them. Nay, he carried his fondness even to inanimate objects, of which we have above set down a pregnant example in his demonstration of love and tenderness towards his boats and ship. He spoke of a ship which he had commanded formerly, and which was long since no more, which he had called the Princess of Brazil, as a widower of a deceased wife. This ship, after having followed the honest business of carrying goods and passengers for hire many years, did at last take to evil courses and turn privateer, in which service, to use his own words, she received many dreadful wounds, which he himself had felt as if they had been his own.

Thursday.—As the wind did not yesterday discover any purpose of shifting, and the water in my belly grew troublesome and rendered me short-breathed, I began a second time to have apprehensions of wanting the assistance of a trochar when none was to be found; I therefore concluded to be tapped again by way of precaution, and accordingly I this morning summoned on board a surgeon from a neighboring parish, one whom the captain greatly recommended, and who did indeed perform his office with much dexterity. He was, I believe, likewise a man of great judgment and knowledge in the profession; but of this I cannot speak with perfect certainty, for, when he was going to open on the dropsy at large and on the particular degree of the distemper under which I labored, I was obliged to stop him short, for the wind was changed, and the captain in the utmost hurry to depart; and to desire him, instead of his opinion, to assist me with his execution. I was now once more delivered from my burden, which was not indeed so great as I had apprehended, wanting two quarts of what was let out at the last operation.

While the surgeon was drawing away my water the sailors were drawing up the anchor; both were finished at the same time; we unfurled our sails and soon passed the Berry-head, which forms the mouth of the bay.

We had not however sailed far when the wind, which, had though with a slow pace, kept us company about six miles, suddenly turned about, and offered to conduct us back again; a favor which, though sorely against the grain, we were obliged to accept.

Nothing remarkable happened this day; for as to the firm persuasion of the captain that he was under the spell of witchcraft, I would not repeat it too often, though indeed he repeated it an hundred times every day; in truth, he talked of nothing else, and seemed not only to be satisfied in general of his being bewitched, but actually to have fixed with good certainty on the person of the witch, whom, had he lived in the days of Sir Matthew Hale, he would have infallibly indicted, and very possibly have hanged, for the detestable sin of witchcraft; but that law, and the whole doctrine that supported it, are now out of fashion; and witches, as a learned divine once chose to express himself, are put down by act of parliament. This witch, in the captain's opinion, was no other than Mrs. Francis of Ryde, who, as he insinuated, out of anger to me for not spending more money in her house than she could produce anything to exchange for, or ally pretense to charge for, had laid this spell on his ship.

Though we were again got near our harbor by three in the afternoon, yet it seemed to require a full hour or more before we could come to our former place of anchoring, or berth, as the captain called it. On this occasion we exemplified one of the few advantages which the travelers by water have over the travelers by land. What would the latter often give for the sight of one of those hospitable mansions where he is assured THAT THERE IS GOOD ENTERTAINMENT FOR MAN AND HORSE; and where both may consequently promise themselves to assuage that hunger which exercise is so sure to raise in a healthy constitution.

At their arrival at this mansion how much happier is the state of the horse than that of the master! The former is immediately led to his repast, such as it is, and, whatever it is, he falls to it with appetite. But the latter is in a much worse situation. His hunger, however violent, is always in some degree delicate, and his food must have some kind of ornament, or, as the more usual phrase is, of dressing, to recommend it. Now all dressing requires time, and therefore, though perhaps the sheep might be just killed before you came to the inn, yet in cutting him up, fetching the joint, which the landlord by mistake said he had in the house, from the butcher at two miles' distance, and afterwards warming it a little by the fire, two hours at least must be consumed, while hunger, for want of better food, preys all the time on the vitals of the man.

How different was the case with us! we carried our provision, our kitchen, and our cook with us, and we were at one and the same time traveling on our road, and sitting down to a repast of fish, with which the greatest table in London can scarce at any rate be supplied.

Friday.—As we were disappointed of our wind, and obliged to return back the preceding evening, we resolved to extract all the good we could out of our misfortune, and to add considerably to our fresh stores of meat and bread, with which we were very indifferently provided when we hurried away yesterday. By the captain's advice we likewise laid in some stores of butter, which we salted and potted ourselves, for our use at Lisbon, and we had great reason afterwards to thank him for his advice.

In the afternoon I persuaded my wife whom it was no easy matter for me to force from my side, to take a walk on shore, whither the gallant captain declared he was ready to attend her. Accordingly the ladies set out, and left me to enjoy a sweet and comfortable nap after the operation of the preceding day.

Thus we enjoyed our separate pleasures full three hours, when we met again, and my wife gave the foregoing account of the gentleman whom I have before compared to Axylus, and of his habitation, to both which she had been introduced by the captain, in the style of an old friend and acquaintance, though this foundation of intimacy seemed to her to be no deeper laid than in an accidental dinner, eaten many years before, at this temple of hospitality, when the captain lay wind-bound in the same bay.

Saturday.—Early this morning the wind seemed inclined to change in our favor. Our alert captain snatched its very first motion, and got under sail with so very gentle a breeze that, as the tide was against him, he recommended to a fishing boy to bring after him a vast salmon and some other provisions which lay ready for him on shore.

Our anchor was up at six, and before nine in the morning we had doubled the Berry-head, and were arrived off Dartmouth, having gone full three miles in as many hours, in direct opposition to the tide, which only befriended us out of our harbor; and though the wind was perhaps our friend, it was so very silent, and exerted itself so little in our favor, that, like some cool partisans, it was difficult to say whether it was with us or against us. The captain, however, declared the former to be the case during the whole three hours; but at last he perceived his error, or rather, perhaps, this friend, which had hitherto wavered in choosing his side, became now more determined. The captain then suddenly tacked about, and, asserting that he was bewitched, submitted to return to the place from whence he came. Now, though I am as free from superstition as any man breathing, and never did believe in witches, notwithstanding all the excellent arguments of my lord chief-justice Hale in their favor, and long before they were put down by act of parliament, yet by what power a ship of burden should sail three miles against both wind and tide, I cannot conceive, unless there was some supernatural interposition in the case; nay, could we admit that the wind stood neuter, the difficulty would still remain. So that we must of necessity conclude that the ship was either bewinded or bewitched. The captain, perhaps, had another meaning. He imagined himself, I believe, bewitched, because the wind, instead of persevering in its change in his favor, for change it certainly did that morning, should suddenly return to its favorite station, and blow him back towards the bay. But, if this was his opinion, he soon saw cause to alter; for he had not measured half the way back when the wind again declared in his favor, and so loudly, that there was no possibility of being mistaken. The orders for the second tack were given, and obeyed with much more alacrity than those had been for the first. We were all of us indeed in high spirits on the occasion; though some of us a little regretted the good things we were likely to leave behind us by the fisherman's neglect; I might give it a worse name, for he faithfully promised to execute the commission, which he had had abundant opportunity to do; but nautica fides deserves as much to be proverbial as ever Punica fides could formerly have done. Nay, when we consider that the Carthaginians came from the Phenicians who are supposed to have produced the first mariners, we may probably see the true reason of the adage, and it may open a field of very curious discoveries to the antiquarian.

We were, however, too eager to pursue our voyage to suffer anything we left behind us to interrupt our happiness, which, indeed, many agreeable circumstances conspired to advance. The weather was inexpressibly pleasant, and we were all seated on the deck, when our canvas began to swell with the wind. We had likewise in our view above thirty other sail around us, all in the same situation. Here an observation occurred to me, which, perhaps, though extremely obvious, did not offer itself to every individual in our little fleet: when I perceived with what different success we proceeded under the influence of a superior power which, while we lay almost idle ourselves, pushed us forward on our intended voyage, and compared this with the slow progress which we had made in the morning, of ourselves, and without any such assistance, I could not help reflecting how often the greatest abilities lie windbound as it were in life; or, if they venture out and attempt to beat the seas, they struggle in vain against wind and tide, and, if they have not sufficient prudence to put back, are most probably cast away on the rocks and quicksands which are every day ready to devour them.

It was now our fortune to set out melioribus avibus. The wind freshened so briskly in our poop that the shore appeared to move from us as fast as we did from the shore. The captain declared he was sure of a wind, meaning its continuance; but he had disappointed us so often that he had lost all credit. However, he kept his word a little better now, and we lost sight of our native land as joyfully, at least, as it is usual to regain it.

Sunday.—The next morning the captain told me he thought himself thirty miles to the westward of Plymouth, and before evening declared that the Lizard Point, which is the extremity of Cornwall, bore several leagues to leeward. Nothing remarkable passed this day, except the captain's devotion, who, in his own phrase, summoned all hands to prayers, which were read by a common sailor upon deck, with more devout force and address than they are commonly read by a country curate, and received with more decency and attention by the sailors than are usually preserved in city congregations. I am indeed assured, that if any such affected disregard of the solemn office in which they were engaged, as I have seen practiced by fine gentlemen and ladies, expressing a kind of apprehension lest they should be suspected of being really in earnest in their devotion, had been shown here, they would have contracted the contempt of the whole audience. To say the truth, from what I observed in the behavior of the sailors in this voyage, and on comparing it with what I have formerly seen of them at sea and on shore, I am convinced that on land there is nothing more idle and dissolute; in their own element there are no persons near the level of their degree who live in the constant practice of half so many good qualities.

They are, for much the greater part, perfect masters of their business, and always extremely alert, and ready in executing it, without any regard to fatigue or hazard. The soldiers themselves are not better disciplined nor more obedient to orders than these whilst aboard; they submit to every difficulty which attends their calling with cheerfulness, and no less virtues and patience and fortitude are exercised by them every day of their lives. All these good qualities, however, they always leave behind them on shipboard; the sailor out of water is, indeed, as wretched an animal as the fish out of water; for though the former hath, in common with amphibious animals, the bare power of existing on the land, yet if he be kept there any time he never fails to become a nuisance. The ship having had a good deal of motion since she was last under sail, our women returned to their sickness, and I to my solitude; having, for twenty-four hours together, scarce opened my lips to a single person. This circumstance of being shut up within the circumference of a few yards, with a score of human creatures, with not one of whom it was possible to converse, was perhaps so rare as scarce ever to have happened before, nor could it ever happen to one who disliked it more than myself, or to myself at a season when I wanted more food for my social disposition, or could converse less wholesomely and happily with my own thoughts. To this accident, which fortune opened to me in the Downs, was owing the first serious thought which I ever entertained of enrolling myself among the voyage-writers; some of the most amusing pages, if, indeed, there be any which deserve that name, were possibly the production of the most disagreeable hours which ever haunted the author.

Monday.—At noon the captain took an observation, by which it appeared that Ushant bore some leagues northward of us, and that we were just entering the bay of Biscay. We had advanced a very few miles in this bay before we were entirely becalmed: we furled our sails, as being of no use to us while we lay in this most disagreeable situation, more detested by the sailors than the most violent tempest: we were alarmed with the loss of a fine piece of salt beef, which had been hung in the sea to freshen it; this being, it seems, the strange property of salt-water. The thief was immediately suspected, and presently afterwards taken by the sailors. He was, indeed, no other than a huge shark, who, not knowing when he was well off, swallowed another piece of beef, together with a great iron crook on which it was hung, and by which he was dragged into the ship. I should scarce have mentioned the catching this shark, though so exactly conformable to the rules and practice of voyage-writing, had it not been for a strange circumstance that attended it. This was the recovery of the stolen beef out of the shark's maw, where it lay unchewed and undigested, and whence, being conveyed into the pot, the flesh, and the thief that had stolen it, joined together in furnishing variety to the ship's crew.

During this calm we likewise found the mast of a large vessel, which the captain thought had lain at least three years in the sea. It was stuck all over with a little shell-fish or reptile, called a barnacle, and which probably are the prey of the rockfish, as our captain calls it, asserting that it is the finest fish in the world; for which we are obliged to confide entirely to his taste; for, though he struck the fish with a kind of harping-iron, and wounded him, I am convinced, to death, yet he could not possess himself of his body; but the poor wretch escaped to linger out a few hours with probably great torments.

In the evening our wind returned, and so briskly, that we ran upwards of twenty leagues before the next day's [Tuesday's] observation, which brought us to lat. 47 degrees 42'. The captain promised us a very speedy passage through the bay; but he deceived us, or the wind deceived him, for it so slackened at sunset, that it scarce carried us a mile in an hour during the whole succeeding night.

Wednesday.—A gale struck up a little after sunrising, which carried us between three and four knots or miles an hour. We were this day at noon about the middle of the bay of Biscay, when the wind once more deserted us, and we were so entirely becalmed, that we did not advance a mile in many hours. My fresh-water reader will perhaps conceive no unpleasant idea from this calm; but it affected us much more than a storm could have done; for, as the irascible passions of men are apt to swell with indignation long after the injury which first raised them is over, so fared it with the sea. It rose mountains high, and lifted our poor ship up and down, backwards and forwards, with so violent an emotion, that there was scarce a man in the ship better able to stand than myself. Every utensil in our cabin rolled up and down, as we should have rolled ourselves, had not our chairs been fast lashed to the floor. In this situation, with our tables likewise fastened by ropes, the captain and myself took our meal with some difficulty, and swallowed a little of our broth, for we spilt much the greater part. The remainder of our dinner being an old, lean, tame duck roasted, I regretted but little the loss of, my teeth not being good enough to have chewed it.

Our women, who began to creep out of their holes in the morning, retired again within the cabin to their beds, and were no more heard of this day, in which my whole comfort was to find by the captain's relation that the swelling was sometimes much worse; he did, indeed, take this occasion to be more communicative than ever, and informed me of such misadventures that had befallen him within forty-six years at sea as might frighten a very bold spirit from undertaking even the shortest voyage. Were these, indeed, but universally known, our matrons of quality would possibly be deterred from venturing their tender offspring at sea; by which means our navy would lose the honor of many a young commodore, who at twenty-two is better versed in maritime affairs than real seamen are made by experience at sixty. And this may, perhaps, appear the more extraordinary, as the education of both seems to be pretty much the same; neither of them having had their courage tried by Virgil's description of a storm, in which, inspired as he was, I doubt whether our captain doth not exceed him. In the evening the wind, which continued in the N.W., again freshened, and that so briskly that Cape Finisterre appeared by this day's observation to bear a few miles to the southward. We now indeed sailed, or rather flew, near ten knots an hour; and the captain, in the redundancy of his good-humor, declared he would go to church at Lisbon on Sunday next, for that he was sure of a wind; and, indeed, we all firmly believed him. But the event again contradicted him; for we were again visited by a calm in the evening.

But here, though our voyage was retarded, we were entertained with a scene, which as no one can behold without going to sea, so no one can form an idea of anything equal to it on shore. We were seated on the deck, women and all, in the serenest evening that can be imagined. Not a single cloud presented itself to our view, and the sun himself was the only object which engrossed our whole attention. He did indeed set with a majesty which is incapable of description, with which, while the horizon was yet blazing with glory, our eyes were called off to the opposite part to survey the moon, which was then at full, and which in rising presented us with the second object that this world hath offered to our vision. Compared to these the pageantry of theaters, or splendor of courts, are sights almost below the regard of children. We did not return from the deck till late in the evening; the weather being inexpressibly pleasant, and so warm that even my old distemper perceived the alteration of the climate. There was indeed a swell, but nothing comparable to what we had felt before, and it affected us on the deck much less than in the cabin.

Friday.—The calm continued till sun-rising, when the wind likewise arose, but unluckily for us it came from a wrong quarter; it was S.S.E., which is that very wind which Juno would have solicited of Aeolus, had Gneas been in our latitude bound for Lisbon.

The captain now put on his most melancholy aspect, and resumed his former opinion that he was bewitched. He declared with great solemnity that this was worse and worse, for that a wind directly in his teeth was worse than no wind at all. Had we pursued the course which the wind persuaded us to take we had gone directly for Newfoundland, if we had not fallen in with Ireland in our way. Two ways remained to avoid this; one was to put into a port of Galicia; the other, to beat to the westward with as little sail as possible: and this was our captain's election.

As for us, poor passengers, any port would have been welcome to us; especially, as not only our fresh provisions, except a great number of old ducks and fowls, but even our bread was come to an end, and nothing but sea-biscuit remained, which I could not chew. So that now for the first time in my life I saw what it was to want a bit of bread.

The wind however was not so unkind as we had apprehended; but, having declined with the sun, it changed at the approach of the moon, and became again favorable to us, though so gentle that the next day's observation carried us very little to the southward of Cape Finisterre. This evening at six the wind, which had been very quiet all day, rose very high, and continuing in our favor drove us seven knots an hour.

This day we saw a sail, the only one, as I heard of, we had seen in our whole passage through the bay. I mention this on account of what appeared to me somewhat extraordinary. Though she was at such a distance that I could only perceive she was a ship, the sailors discovered that she was a snow, bound to a port in Galicia.

Sunday.—After prayers, which our good captain read on the deck with an audible voice, and with but one mistake, of a lion for Elias, in the second lesson for this day, we found ourselves far advanced in 42 degrees, and the captain declared we should sup off Porte. We had not much wind this day; but, as this was directly in our favor, we made it up with sail, of which we crowded all we had. We went only at the rate of four miles an hour, but with so uneasy a motion, continuing rolling from side to side, that I suffered more than I had done in our whole voyage; my bowels being almost twisted out of my belly. However, the day was very serene and bright, and the captain, who was in high spirits, affirmed he had never passed a pleasanter at sea.

The wind continued so brisk that we ran upward of six knots an hour the whole night.

Monday.—In the morning our captain concluded that he was got into lat. 40 degrees, and was very little short of the Burlings, as they are called in the charts. We came up with them at five in the afternoon, being the first land we had distinctly seen since we left Devonshire. They consist of abundance of little rocky islands, a little distant from the shore, three of them only showing themselves above the water.

Here the Portuguese maintain a kind of garrison, if we may allow it that name. It consists of malefactors, who are banished hither for a term, for divers small offenses—a policy which they may have copied from the Egyptians, as we may read in Diodorus Siculus. That wise people, to prevent the corruption of good manners by evil communication, built a town on the Red Sea, whither they transported a great number of their criminals, having first set an indelible mark on them, to prevent their returning and mixing with the sober part of their citizens. These rocks lie about fifteen leagues northwest of Cape Roxent, or, as it is commonly called, the Rock of Lisbon, which we passed early the next morning. The wind, indeed, would have carried us thither sooner; but the captain was not in a hurry, as he was to lose nothing by his delay.

Tuesday.—This is a very high mountain, situated on the northern side of the mouth of the river Tajo, which, rising about Madrid, in Spain, and soon becoming navigable for small craft, empties itself, after a long course, into the sea, about four leagues below Lisbon.

On the summit of the rock stands a hermitage, which is now in the possession of an Englishman, who was formerly master of a vessel trading to Lisbon; and, having changed his religion and his manners, the latter of which, at least, were none of the best, betook himself to this place, in order to do penance for his sins. He is now very old, and hath inhabited this hermitage for a great number of years, during which he hath received some countenance from the royal family, and particularly from the present queen dowager, whose piety refuses no trouble or expense by which she may make a proselyte, being used to say that the saving one soul would repay all the endeavors of her life. Here we waited for the tide, and had the pleasure of surveying the face of the country, the soil of which, at this season, exactly resembles an old brick-kiln, or a field where the green sward is pared up and set a-burning, or rather a smoking, in little heaps to manure the land. This sight will, perhaps, of all others, make an Englishman proud of, and pleased with, his own country, which in verdure excels, I believe, every other country. Another deficiency here is the want of large trees, nothing above a shrub being here to be discovered in the circumference of many miles.

At this place we took a pilot on board, who, being the first Portuguese we spoke to, gave us an instance of that religious observance which is paid by all nations to their laws; for, whereas it is here a capital offense to assist any person in going on shore from a foreign vessel before it hath been examined, and every person in it viewed by the magistrates of health, as they are called, this worthy pilot, for a very small reward, rowed the Portuguese priest to shore at this place, beyond which he did not dare to advance, and in venturing whither he had given sufficient testimony of love for his native country.

We did not enter the Tajo till noon, when, after passing several old castles and other buildings which had greatly the aspect of ruins, we came to the castle of Bellisle, where we had a full prospect of Lisbon, and were, indeed, within three miles of it.

Here we were saluted with a gun, which was a signal to pass no farther till we had complied with certain ceremonies which the laws of this country require to be observed by all ships which arrive in this port. We were obliged then to cast anchor, and expect the arrival of the officers of the customs, without whose passport no ship must proceed farther than this place.

Here likewise we received a visit from one of those magistrates of health before mentioned. He refused to come on board the ship till every person in her had been drawn up on deck and personally viewed by him. This occasioned some delay on my part, as it was not the work of a minute to lift me from the cabin to the deck. The captain thought my particular case might have been excused from this ceremony, and that it would be abundantly sufficient if the magistrate, who was obliged afterwards to visit the cabin, surveyed me there. But this did not satisfy the magistrate's strict regard to his duty. When he was told of my lameness, he called out, with a voice of authority, "Let him be brought up," and his orders were presently complied with. He was, indeed, a person of great dignity, as well as of the most exact fidelity in the discharge of his trust. Both which are the more admirable as his salary is less than thirty pounds English per annum.

Before a ship hath been visited by one of those magistrates no person can lawfully go on board her, nor can any on board depart from her. This I saw exemplified in a remarkable instance. The young lad whom I have mentioned as one of our passengers was here met by his father, who, on the first news of the captain's arrival, came from Lisbon to Bellisle in a boat, being eager to embrace a son whom he had not seen for many years. But when he came alongside our ship neither did the father dare ascend nor the son descend, as the magistrate of health had not yet been on board. Some of our readers will, perhaps, admire the great caution of this policy, so nicely calculated for the preservation of this country from all pestilential distempers. Others will as probably regard it as too exact and formal to be constantly persisted in, in seasons of the utmost safety, as well as in times of danger. I will not decide either way, but will content myself with observing that I never yet saw or heard of a place where a traveler had so much trouble given him at his landing as here. The only use of which, as all such matters begin and end in form only, is to put it into the power of low and mean fellows to be either rudely officious or grossly corrupt, as they shall see occasion to prefer the gratification of their pride or of their avarice.

Of this kind, likewise, is that power which is lodged with other officers here, of taking away every grain of snuff and every leaf of tobacco brought hither from other countries, though only for the temporary use of the person during his residence here. This is executed with great insolence, and, as it is in the hands of the dregs of the people, very scandalously; for, under pretense of searching for tobacco and snuff, they are sure to steal whatever they can find, insomuch that when they came on board our sailors addressed us in the Covent-garden language: "Pray, gentlemen and ladies, take care of your swords and watches." Indeed, I never yet saw anything equal to the contempt and hatred which our honest tars every moment expressed for these Portuguese officers.

At Bellisle lies buried Catharine of Arragon, widow of prince Arthur, eldest son of our Henry VII, afterwards married to, and divorced from Henry VIII. Close by the church where her remains are deposited is a large convent of Geronymites, one of the most beautiful piles of building in all Portugal.

In the evening, at twelve, our ship, having received previous visits from all the necessary parties, took the advantage of the tide, and having sailed up to Lisbon cast anchor there, in a calm and moonshiny night, which made the passage incredibly pleasant to the women, who remained three hours enjoying it, whilst I was left to the cooler transports of enjoying their pleasures at second-hand; and yet, cooler as they may be, whoever is totally ignorant of such sensation is, at the same time, void of all ideas of friendship.

Wednesday.—Lisbon, before which we now lay at anchor, is said to be built on the same number of hills with old Rome; but these do not all appear to the water; on the contrary, one sees from thence one vast high hill and rock, with buildings arising above one another, and that in so steep and almost perpendicular a manner, that they all seem to have but one foundation.

As the houses, convents, churches, etc., are large, and all built with white stone, they look very beautiful at a distance; but as you approach nearer, and find them to want every kind of ornament, all idea of beauty vanishes at once. While I was surveying the prospect of this city, which bears so little resemblance to any other that I have ever seen, a reflection occurred to me that, if a man was suddenly to be removed from Palmyra hither, and should take a view of no other city, in how glorious a light would the ancient architecture appear to him! and what desolation and destruction of arts and sciences would he conclude had happened between the several eras of these cities!

I had now waited full three hours upon deck for the return of my man, whom I had sent to bespeak a good dinner (a thing which had been long unknown to me) on shore, and then to bring a Lisbon chaise with him to the seashore; but it seems the impertinence of the providore was not yet brought to a conclusion. At three o'clock, when I was from emptiness, rather faint than hungry, my man returned, and told me there was a new law lately made that no passenger should set his foot on shore without a special order from the providore, and that he himself would have been sent to prison for disobeying it, had he not been protected as the servant of the captain. He informed me likewise that the captain had been very industrious to get this order, but that it was then the providore's hour of sleep, a time when no man, except the king himself, durst disturb him.

To avoid prolixity, though in a part of my narrative which may be more agreeable to my reader than it was to me, the providore, having at last finished his nap, dispatched this absurd matter of form, and gave me leave to come, or rather to be carried, on shore.

What it was that gave the first hint of this strange law is not easy to guess. Possibly, in the infancy of their defection, and before their government could be well established, they were willing to guard against the bare possibility of surprise, of the success of which bare possibility the Trojan horse will remain for ever on record, as a great and memorable example. Now the Portuguese have no walls to secure them, and a vessel of two or three hundred tons will contain a much larger body of troops than could be concealed in that famous machine, though Virgil tells us (somewhat hyperbolically, I believe) that it was as big as a mountain.

About seven in the evening I got into a chaise on shore, and was driven through the nastiest city in the world, though at the same time one of the most populous, to a kind of coffee-house, which is very pleasantly situated on the brow of a hill, about a mile from the city, and hath a very fine prospect of the river Tajo from Lisbon to the sea. Here we regaled ourselves with a good supper, for which we were as well charged as if the bill had been made on the Bath-road, between Newbury and London.

> And now we could joyfully say,
> Egressi optata Troes potiuntur arena.
> Therefore, in the words of Horace,
> —hie Finis chartaeque viaeque.

Printed in the United Kingdom
by Lightning Source UK Ltd.
136110UK00002B/188/P